THE DIMMING OF AMERICA

Figure 1. The Dynamics of the Dimming of America.

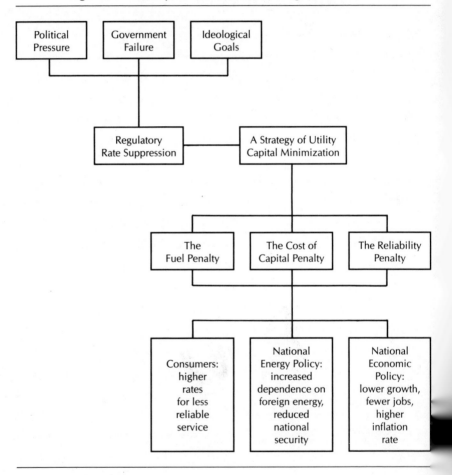

THE DIMMING OF AMERICA
The Real Costs of Electric Utility Regulatory Failure

PETER NAVARRO

BALLINGER PUBLISHING COMPANY
Cambridge, Massachusetts
A Subsidiary of Harper & Row, Publishers, Inc.

International Standard Book Number: 0-88410-945-3

Library of Congress Catalog Card Number: 84-16925

Printed in the United States of America

Library of Congress Cataloging in Publication Data

Navarro, Peter.
    The Dimming of America.

    Bibliography: p.
    Includes index.
    1. Electric utilities—Government policy—United States. I. Title.
HD9685.U5N38 1984 5   363.6'2'0973   84-16925
ISBN 0-88410-945-3

To the Brobergs

CONTENTS

vii

List of Figures

List of Tables

FOREWORD

It has sometimes been said that in a democracy the people get the kind of government they deserve. What is certainly more true, as this volume so well demonstrates, is that in a democracy the people get the kind of regulatory system they deserve. In this brief and disarming book, Mr. Navarro ably analyzes the syndrome of regulatory perversity: utility regulation which provides, in his words, "a perfect paradigm of how and why things go wrong in the American political economy."

Public utility regulation in America has historically been based upon certain presuppositions: 1) that the utility industry is vested with a public interest; 2) that the individual utility has an obligation, in light of its monopoly within a service area, to provide sufficient electric power for all users; 3) that in light of its provision on a monopoly basis of an essential public service, its profits should be limited to a fair return on a fair value – or in the more recent formulation, to a rate of return that would assure an adequate flow of capital.

In light of the long lead-times and immense investment required to provide new generating capacity, as well as the industry's responsibilities and the nature of the regulatory process, the utility industry has been marked as the one *preeminently requiring stability*. Reasonable predictability became the instrument by which to reconcile under conditions of regulation the obligation to users (of adequate capacity) and the obligation to stockholders. Moreover, both stability and predictability have in turn rested upon the absence of inflation, i.e., a stable value of money. And on that stability in money values has rested all the assumptions regarding regulatory ratemaking, the tax system, and even the flow of resources from the capital markets.

In recent years this industry, dependent as it is upon stability, has been forced to contend with the dramatic and unanticipated changes that Mr. Navarro documents. It has been staggered, if not overwhelmed, by a concatenation of events that could not be foreseen during the period in which the norms of the regulatory process were established. It has been forced to contend with exploding fuel costs, general inflation, rapidly changing environmental and safety requirements, escalating capital requirements for new plants, quite inadequate treatment of construction work in progress under conditions of inflation and/or rising real interest rates, a tax system which has driven the real return on equity below zero, and, finally, new technologies that have stressed an industry structure that had been acceptable prior to the nuclear era. For a regulated industry dependent upon reasonable stability, it should come as no surprise that it has come close to being overwhelmed. Perhaps, also, it is no surprise that the political process has tended to pummel the victim of these stunning developments.

The consequences of this radical change in groundrules have perhaps been inevitable. And Mr. Navarro documents these developments with all of the inevitability of a Greek tragedy. The basic proposition is both simple and stark: public utility commissions responding to direct political, institutional, and ideological pressures have suppressed rates in a way that precludes returns adequate[1] to maintain a flow of capital sufficient to provide suitable capacity expeditiously and economically. Utilities have been unable to raise capital save on terms unfair to their stockholders.

After an initial period of disbelief—and of abiding trust in the traditional norms of ratemaking—utilities have come to accept the unpleasant reality that they can no longer fulfill their obligations to both their stockholders and their customers. In the face of rate suppression and of retrospective second-guessing by PUCs of earlier

---

1. It is noteworthy that the initial intervention of the U.S. Department of Energy in ratemaking proceedings was in support of higher rates.

decisions, utilities have adopted a new strategy of capital minimization—of avoiding new commitments to capital outlays whenever possible. Utilities have ultimately preferred to avoid the risks to their shareholders of providing growing capacity—and, consequently to accept the risks to their customers of providing insufficient capacity to meet growing demand. The result is that the industry has turned a blind eye to the now emerging reality of capacity requirements, and is understating, subliminally if not deliberately, these capacity requirements.

Yet, in light of the dramatic changes of the foundations on which the industry has rested, we should scarcely be surprised that performance has also changed. Both the recession and the changed structure of the market may have provided, at least for the moment, ample reserve capacity. But that reserve capacity is melting away, and future troubles are steadily brewing. The cloud on the horizon grows—as it draws steadily closer. Unless we in this nation change our ways, around the end of the decade the likely, if not inevitable, result will be hand-to-mouth provision of required electric power supplies, if not the actual Dimming of America.

Inadequate attention now to those problems that changed conditions have imposed upon both the industry and utility ratemaking, means more problems later on. It means more imported oil and more vulnerability. It means higher returns for bondholders and, paradoxically, eventually stockholders as well. In the end, it means higher rates for the ratepayers. The great irony, of course, is that such outcomes were surely not the intent of the existing regulatory system.

Who can possibly benefit from such a morass? After all, it's an ill wind that blows nobody any good. As in the case of the defective and outmoded system of natural gas regulation that existed under the Phillips regime, the principal beneficiaries are likely to be Canadian exporters of electric power. However welcome that news may be to our Northern neighbors, it adds to the difficulties of America's balance of payments already under severe duress.

There may be a parallel here to the large-scale Federal deficits and the rapidly burgeoning national debt. In recent years this nation has fallen prey to the illusion that somehow or other we could maintain our social programs, pay growing interest on the national debt, and expand our national defenses while *lowering* taxes. By parallel we have come to believe that we can steadily expand generating capacity while *suppressing* power rates. And, just as there is no fiscal gimmickry that can resolve the nation's budgetary dilemma, similarly there is no regulatory gimmickry that can provide the necessary electric generating capacity while holding down rates. In utility regulation, as in budget making, we shall have to recognize that there is a day of reckoning.

The final paradox is that the utility industry, on which we depend for expanding our supplies of electric energy, is now an industry that cannot stand good news. National prosperity implies both steadily expanding power requirements and (with such large federal deficits) steadily rising real interest rates which make the provision of the required capacity ever more unattainable. Is this the outcome that the American democracy deserves—or desires?

—James R. Schlesinger

PREFACE

People often ask me how I came to study electric utility regulation. Their queries are always made in a tone that implies that the topic is other than a "sexy," scintillating, or intellectually exciting one. My stock reply is that for anyone intrigued by the politics and the economics of regulation, few subjects surpass electric utility regulation for higher education in the perversity, pitfalls, and practice of the regulatory art and science.

I first tackled the subject shortly after the 1973–74 Arab oil embargo. Then in the employ of the Department of Energy (DOE), I was assigned the task of explaining why the electric utility industry continued to consume expensive imported oil at a rate that not only threatened national security but also seemingly defied economic logic. Probing behind the veil of utility regulation, I discovered what has turned out to be a perfect paradigm of how and why things go wrong in the American political economy. Indeed, all the ingredients of regulatory failure are present in the electric utility industry: short-run and short-sighted politically expedient decisions, inadequate government institutions, and, most subtly, misguided ideology.

The consequences of this regulatory failure go far beyond DOE's concern about America's crippling oil import dependence. Indeed, regulatory failure promises electricity consumers a bleak future of higher rates for less reliable service at the same time that it threatens to erode the very foundations of our economic growth and prosperity.

This book is the culmination of seven years of work fleshing out the causes and consequences of the electric utility regulatory conundrum. It is a *nontechnical* synthesis of extensive research and numerous academic articles. It is written in a style designed to reach out to every interested layperson—from electricity consumers and utility shareholders to business persons, policymakers, and pundits; its aim is a thorough description of a dramatic and important problem.

This nontechnical synthesis is based in part on my technical articles, and I therefore must thank the various magazines and journals that have published them. These include the *Bell Journal of Economics, Energy Journal, Energy Law Journal, Financial Analysts Journal, Harvard Business Review, Public Interest, Public Utilities Fortnightly,* and *Regulation.* I would also like to thank the *Wall Street Journal* and *Business Week* for their timely publication of several articles on the relationship of utility regulation and national policy goals.

My gratitude must also go to those scholars, primarily in the Harvard community, who offered valuable comments and criticism of my research: Richard Caves, Dale Jorgenson, Thomas Stauffer, Joseph Kalt, Henry Lee, and William Hogan. And I would like to thank Jeffrey Dubin of the California Institute of Technology, who coauthored the paper on which a portion of Chapter 4 is based, and Michael Crew of Rutgers University, who edited the book *Regulatory Reform and Public Utilities,* in which that article appeared.

Over the past five years the DOE funded a large share of the technical research that forms the backbone of this book. At DOE, J. Steven Herod, director of the Office of Electrical Systems, stands out as a gentleman and scholar who threatens to give the term bureaucrat a good name. The epitome of the dedicated public servant, Mr. Herod was a constant source of information, insight, and inspiration. His colleagues Jeffrey Skeer and Tom Grahame also deserve special mention and thanks.

I am likewise grateful to a number of organizations and firms in the private sector that have contributed research grants to Harvard University on my behalf. These private-sector contributors include PPG Industries, American Electric Power, Bechtel Corporation, Carolina Power and Light, Edison Electric Institute, Iowa Public

Service Company, New England Electric Systems, and Philadelphia Electric Company.

And now kudos to my research team: Vlad Jenkins, Eric Brynjolfsen, Menzie Chinn, Larry Alberts, Louise Sheiner, and Robert Kornfeld. Celia Shneider, Maureen Williams, Jane E. Williams, Barbara Hamwey, and Julie A. Fernandez performed typing and word processing for this book and the technical articles. Wynne Cougill, my able editor since day one of my writing career, performed her usual yeoman duty helping to edit the manuscript. Margaret Stock shepherded the manuscript through its final stages.

But my biggest thanks go to two very special people. First, Professor Malcolm Harris of the University of Connecticut has acted as critical reader, coauthor on other papers, and close friend over a five-year period. A former regulator and now a professor of finance at the University of Connecticut, Malcolm possesses a rare combination of academic knowledge, technical expertise, and hands-on experience. Ever cheerful and incredibly hardworking, he and his good humor helped me and my research assistants through many an all-night session at Harvard's well-equipped but drab and smoky computer room.

Last, but hardly least, there is Geraldine Willigan. An editor at the *Harvard Business Review*, Geri worked tirelessly on the manuscript to make it readable for the broadest possible audience. Her contributions to the book include not only substantive editing but also active participation in some of the early drafting. Without her, this book literally would not exist.

Two disclaimers remain to be stated. First, the opinions and conclusions in this book are entirely my own. That said, I must deeply thank the Energy and Environmental Policy Center at Harvard University's Kennedy School of Government. The EEPC has provided me with a wonderful place to work, published many of my articles first as discussion papers, administered my research grants, and, above all, provided a stimulating, intellectual atmosphere in which to conduct research. In this regard, the Executive Director Henry Lee deserves my warmest gratitude, as does Kathleen Jervey.

Second, while this book unquestionably is an indictment of the regulatory process, it should in no way be construed as a criticism of the regulators themselves. I have nothing but the highest regard for the extremely dedicated (and typically underpaid) men and women who

toil as commissioners and staff members in state public utility commis-
as commissioners and staff members in state public utility commissions across this nation. I also have a deep sympathy for these public
servants; theirs is a thankless job, prone to failure not because of their
shortcomings but because of what we shall see are the political,
institutional, and ideological storms that swirl around them.

INTRODUCTION

The electric utility industry is the energy cornerstone of the American economy. After a century of continual innovation and steady expansion, this industry now provides one-fourth of the power used by our homes, one-third of that used by our stores and businesses, and one-seventh of that used by our nation's factories and industries; its power plants and equipment comprise over one-fifth of the nation's invested industrial capital.[1]

America's electricity supply is among the world's most reliable: With the flick of a switch, electricity feeds our vacuum cleaners, air conditioners, televisions, and stoves; it services our hospitals and schools; it lights our neighborhood playgrounds and streets; and it provides jobs and income for tens of millions of Americans. It is there when we need or want it, making our lives more comfortable, convenient, and in some cases, simply possible.

At the same time that it supports the nation's current high standard of living, electricity also promises to be the energy springboard for our future growth and prosperity. Already it serves as the basis

1. National Energy Policy Plan (NEPP) figures for 1982 proportion of end use satisfied by electricity; financial data from U.S. Department of Energy, Energy Information Administration, "Impacts of Financial Constraints on the Electric Utility Industry," EIA-0311, December 1981, p. 7.

for a wide variety of productivity-enhancing technological innovations and industrial devices, ranging from computers and robots to electric arc furnaces, advanced metallurgical processors, and lasers. It is revolutionizing such fields as telecommunications, transportation, agricultural irrigation, and food processing.

Unfortunately, after more than a decade of rapidly rising energy and capital costs, the electricity cornerstone is now threatened. Amidst the falling stock prices and bond ratings of a once blue-chip industry, the dimming of America—in the sense of massive electricity shortages and stoppages—has been predicted. We shall see throughout this book that such warnings may be unduly alarmist, but that there is a great danger of a more figurative dimming of America. In this electricity future—which can be avoided—we may face the possibility of needlessly high electric rates, an unnecessary and increasing reliance on foreign energy, and reduced economic growth. A remote possibility also exists—in some regions of the country more than others—of periodic electricity shortages and, in the worst-case scenarios, resultant blackouts, rolling brownouts, and electricity rationing.

Driving America toward this dim future is a greatly flawed system of electric utility regulation, which, for a multitude of largely misunderstood reasons, is unable to keep pace with abrupt and rapid changes in energy and capital costs and equally jolting changes in energy demand and use patterns. The result of this regulatory failure is "rate suppression," a pernicious phenomenon marked by electricity rates that continually rise but never fast enough to cover the true and steadily escalating costs of generating electricity. As a result of this phenomenon, and despite the fact that electricity rates have more than tripled since the early 1970s, many utilities have seen their real earnings cut almost in half.

In response to such rate suppression and the attendant erosion of utility earnings, today's electric utility executives have been increasingly turning to a "strategy of capital minimization." That is, because of new financial constraints, utility managers have been dramatically cutting back on the capital investments that are necessary to keep the lights on and rates as low as possible. These foregone investments include those that should have been made for reliability reasons (primarily new power plants to meet load growth) as well as those that are economic and so would cut consumers' electricity bills (projects ranging from coal conversion to conservation). Today, because of regulatory constraints, such investments are, from the utility executive's point of view, either financially unsound or financially impossible.

Why and how have electric utility regulators been suppressing electricity rates, and why and how are utility executives in turn foregoing necessary and economic investments that are in the interests of both their customers and the nation? What will be the costs of this all-too-subtle rate-suppression/capital-minimization syndrome? Will the lights actually go out, or is the greater, more subtle threat an economic one that targets consumer pocketbooks and any new era of American prosperity? This book is intended to provide a framework for answering these questions. At the same time, it presents a detailed blueprint for constructive policy reforms designed to prevent the dimming of America.

Part I examines the phenomenon of rate suppression within the context of the regulatory mandate that state public utility commissions are supposed to obey. It goes on to show how a strategy of capital minimization results from rate suppression because of the utility executive's twin and often conflicting responsibilities to consumers and shareholders.

Part II discusses the many ways that capital minimization can manifest itself, from a utility's failure to build new power plants or to convert existing noneconomic oil plants to coal to its unwillingness to pursue sufficient investment in energy conservation and alternative energy resources, such as wind and solar. It then illustrates how minimizing capital expenditures creates "fuel, cost of capital, and reliability penalties," which ultimately must be borne not only by the utilities and their stockholders but also by ratepayers and the nation.

Part III elaborates on, and in some cases quantifies, these three regulatory penalties and demonstrates their costly and paradoxical effects first on national economic and energy policy goals and then on electricity consumers.

The book concludes with a policy blueprint for reforming this potentially dangerous, but by no means irreversible, situation. The hope is that this book will steer our electric utility industry onto a path that better serves all our interests.

THE REGULATORS VERSUS THE UTILITIES

Regulatory Rate Suppression		A Strategy of Utility Capital Minimization

1 REGULATORY RATE SUPPRESSION

The dimming of America is being foreshadowed by the dramatic financial deterioration the electric utility industry has experienced over the past decade; it has its roots deep in a pernicious phenomenon known as "regulatory rate suppression." Simply stated, regulatory rate suppression refers to the fact that since the early 1970s, regulated electricity prices have by and large failed to reflect the true market cost of generating electricity. The reason for this is a regulatory failure widespread among the state public utility commissions that set electricity prices.

ORIGINS OF THE PUCs

Today state public utility commissions (PUCs) regulate the more than 150 investor-owned utilities that supply America with over 80 percent of its electricity and from whom virtually all of the future increases in supply will come. (The remaining 20 percent is supplied primarily by rural cooperatives and public entities ranging from the federal government's Tennessee Valley and Bonneville Power authorities to state- and city-run cooperatives.)

Such PUC regulation has its origins in the Populist and Progressive movements of the late 1800s and early 1900s. During that era, the

3

Industrial Revolution was in full bloom, as were widespread abuses by American business interests. Robber barons like Jay Gould and Henry Villard frequently made headlines with multimillion-dollar stock swindles, while empire builders like John D. Rockefeller gobbled up smaller competitors and fed a burgeoning number of monopolistic corporate trusts.

At the same time, the nation's growing water, gas, telephone, and electric utilities were sometimes discovered with their hands in the government till or reaching deep into their customers' pockets. In 1905, for example, a New York state legislative investigation committee found that Consolidated Gas charged New York City $80,000 for the same amount of electricity for which it charged its private customers only $25,000, while New York Gas and Electric was discovered charging its customers an average of 8 cents per kilowatt hour for electricity that cost less than half that much to produce.[1]

With such corporate abuses running rampant, public mistrust of the unbridled power of "big business" reached unprecedented heights. Out of this public mistrust—skillfully transformed into political action by Populist and Progressive leaders—emerged the widest range of government interventions into the American economy ever witnessed.

At the federal level, antitrust laws like the Sherman and Clayton Acts were passed to curb monopoly practices and to stem the tide of corporate mergers. At the same time, a veritable army of agencies was established to regulate industries where some of the worst abuses had been observed. The Interstate Commerce Commission, for example, was formed to control the octopus railroads, while the Commodities Exchange Commission was set up to monitor that wild and woolly arena of speculation and fraud, the stock market.

At the state level, and as part of this overall trustbusting trend, the Progressives began to put the nation's private utilities under public control (hence the somewhat misleading term *public utilities* for these private, investor-owned corporations).

In 1907, in large part because of the uncovering of the abuses previously mentioned, the New York state legislature created a public utility commission to supervise its electric and gas utilities. In that same year, Wisconsin, at the urging of the well-known Progressive leader Robert LaFollette, followed suit. A year later Vermont formed such a commission, and Maryland was next. By 1930 every state but

1. Douglas Anderson, *Regulatory Policies and Electric Utilities* (Boston: Auburn House, 1981), pp. 48–51.

Delaware and Texas had established a PUC. (Delaware and Texas established PUCs in 1949 and 1975, respectively.) Under the state charters, these commissions were given broad powers to regulate "in the public interest." Today PUCs set electricity prices for the 1.8 trillion kilowatt hours the nation's investor-owned utilities generate annually.

THE REGULATORY BARGAIN

As it has since been translated into the language of economics, the Populist/Progressive rationale for PUC regulation represents a classic statement of the "natural monopoly" argument for government intervention. In the case of electric utilities, the argument goes like this.

Electricity generation is generally characterized by "economies of scale": For the most part, the larger the power plant, the cheaper it is to generate a unit of electricity. Because of these economies of scale, a free market in electricity typically will lead to a situation of "natural monopoly"; that is, one large utility with the lowest costs will eventually drive out its smaller rivals through lower prices.[2] Once this large utility corners its market, consumers are at the mercy of a mammoth, price-gouging monopolist.

At the same time, the supply of electricity to consumers is characterized by "economies of distribution." This means that it is cheaper for one utility to provide the wires, poles, and hookups for a service area than it is for many utilities to supply redundant equipment.

Thus, while economies of scale tend to create natural monopolies in the electric utility industry, economies of distribution make such a monopolistic structure sensible. But without government intervention, the lack of competition is likely to lead to an inefficient outcome. As economists beginning with Adam Smith have taught us, the inevitable result of such a crippling of the market's "invisible hand" is that the natural monopolist produces too little of the good and charges consumers too high a price for it. Accordingly, it is argued that to preserve economic efficiency, the more "visible foot"

2. Not all economists accept this argument. The question of whether it is valid, however, should not obscure the fact that this rationale has been a primary justification for PUC regulation.

of the government must come in and correct the natural monopoly problem.

From among many proposed alternatives—including franchising, licensing, and public ownership—"rate of return" regulation was chosen by the states to solve the natural monopoly problem, and the PUCs were chartered to administer this regulatory arrangement, the essence of which is as follows.[3] Each utility is granted a monopoly in a particular service area—say, the city of Boston or the southern half of Nevada—and for that privilege agrees to provide low-cost and reliable service to its customers in whatever quantities they demand. In turn, the PUC is obligated to set rates that are high enough to allow the utility the opportunity to earn a "fair and reasonable" return on its investment. As set forth in several important Supreme Court decisions, this "fair and reasonable" doctrine has been interpreted as a *capital attraction standard*: A utility must have the opportunity to earn its market cost of capital on both its new and existing plants so that it is able to attract investors to buy its stocks and bonds and so that it maintains its financial integrity.[4]

To the extent that a PUC denies a utility this opportunity, its regulation is said to be rate suppressive. This suppression manifests itself first as electricity rates that are set too low by the PUC and eventually as a rate of return on investment that falls below the utility's market cost of capital.

A NEW ERA OF RATE SUPPRESSION

For over seventy years, the regulatory bargain between the PUCs and the utilities worked well. The electric utility industry, in particular, enjoyed a virtually uninterrupted period of prosperity and steady growth. Because of economies of scale and evolving technology, the costs of electricity generation generally fell. So, too, did the real cost of electricity to consumers—even as utility profits climbed ever upward.

---

3. Both franchising and licensing are more market-oriented solutions to the problem of natural monopoly than is the bureaucracy-laden regulatory-commission approach. These options, which conservatives have proposed as alternatives to PUC regulation, have been successful in the cable television market, for example.

4. The relevant Supreme Court decisions are *Bluefield Co.* v. *Public Service Commission*, 262 U.S. 679 (1922) and *Federal Power Commission* v. *Hope Natural Gas Co.*, 320 U.S. 591 (1944).

At the same time, the industry provided some of the safest and most reliable power in the world.

By 1950 the industry's assets were worth $20 billion dollars, and by 1960 double that amount.[5] Between 1960 and 1970 utility assets doubled yet again as power plant construction boomed.[6]

Throughout this period of unparalleled expansion, the utility industry consistently passed its capital-attraction test. That is, it earned rates of return on its investment equal to, and in some cases even above, its market cost of capital. Throughout the 1960s, for example, the industry earned a real return on its common equity of around 6 percent.[7] This average return closely paralleled the return of other industrial stocks of the *Fortune* "500" corporations and was at a level that Wall Street analysts agreed represented the industry's capital costs. As a result, investors considered utility stocks and bonds to be the bluest of the blue chips.

Beginning in the 1970s, however, the regulatory arrangement between the PUCs and the utilities began to break down. The catalyst for this regulatory failure was a dramatic rise in both energy and capital costs, two inputs that account for most of a utility's costs of producing electricity. The rise in the costs of these two important ingredients of electricity production was precipitated by four major shocks to the U.S. economy.

The first shock came in the late 1960s in the form of a general and precipitous rise in the rate of inflation brought about primarily by Lyndon Johnson's well-publicized refusal to cut back on social spending for his Great Society programs despite the heavy financial burden the Vietnam War imposed. This refusal to trade off butter for guns (ratified by the Federal Reserve and Treasury printing press) sent the U.S.—and later the world—inflation rate off on a roller-coaster ride that still hasn't completely stopped. Large government budget deficits, the pressure of war financing, and the consequent inflation affected the electric utility industry particularly badly as its capital costs started to ratchet upward.

5. *Moody's Public Utility Manual* (New York: Moody's Investor Service, 1982).

6. Ibid.

7. The real return is equal to the actual, or "nominal," return minus the effects of inflation. In an inflationary economy such as ours, the real return is the best way to gauge a company's earnings. Suppose a firm earns a 13 percent nominal return; if inflation is 7 percent, then its real return is about 6 percent. On the other hand, if inflation is as low as 2 percent or as high as 12 percent, the firm's real return would be about 11 percent or 1 percent, respectively.

A second cost shock quickly followed after the publication of Rachel Carson's *Silent Spring*. That book issued a warning that helped raise the nation's consciousness about widespread environmental degradation, including the then considerable pollution emitted by coal- and oil-fired utility power plants. One form this new awareness took was passage of a tough new Clean Air Act, which required the utility industry to provide not only some of the world's safest and most reliable power but also, henceforth, some of the cleanest. Through numerous amendments enacted over several sessions of Congress and through rulemakings by the Environmental Protection Agency, the federal government sought to achieve that broad goal by requiring the installation of sophisticated and expensive pollution-control technologies and by forcing utilities to burn cleaner though more expensive fuel. While these regulations succeeded in dramatically reducing air pollution, they have raised the cost of building and operating a power plant by as much as 25 percent.[8]

These first two shocks sent unsettling tremors through the capital-intensive utility industry, but the 1973–74 Arab oil embargo and the consequent fourfold increase in petroleum prices caused a major earthquake. While the costs of all forms of energy (including, for example, coal and uranium) rose with the OPEC price shocks, petroleum-dependent utilities were particularly hard hit. Nowhere was the damage more evident than in the Northeast, where, ironically, just a few years earlier many utilities had invested heavily in converting their coal plants to oil in order to comply with the stipulations of the newly legislated Clean Air Act. (When national priorities shifted once again, the federal government immediately attempted to order these utilities back to coal to cut OPEC imports.)[9]

Utilities that sought to avoid the brunt of the OPEC price hikes by building more nuclear plants found themselves set up for a fourth major shock. In the wake of the 1979 incident at Three Mile Island, the Nuclear Regulatory Commission greatly tightened nuclear power plant safety standards. This tightening not only increased the invest-

---

8. For a discussion, see Peter Navarro, "The Politics of Air Pollution," *Public Interest 59*, (Spring 1980): 36.

9. The Energy Supply and Environmental Coordination Act of 1974 ordered those utilities capable of using coal to make the switch. The Powerplant and Industrial Fuel Use Act of 1978 told utilities burning oil or gas to convert their facilities to coal and banned gas burning by utilities starting in 1990.

ment and operating costs of existing nuclear units by requiring substantial retrofitting and new safety procedures but also increased the cost of finishing nuclear plants under construction. In the latter case, costs climbed partly because the new standards created delays while they were being interpreted and partly because they required additional equipment and measures, such as increased reinforcement of the reactor vessel. In 1972, building a nuclear plant cost $208 per kilowatt hour; by 1982 the cost averaged $966 per kwh.[10] More broadly, new regulatory requirements for nuclear plants promulgated during the 1970s have, according to utility analyst Scott A. Fenn and the Atomic Industrial Forum, "approximately doubled the amounts of labor, materials, and equipment and tripled the design engineering effort required for each new unit of nuclear capacity."[11]

Together these four economic shocks dramatically raised the costs of energy and capital to the electric utility industry. At the same time, conventional power plant technologies reached apparent limits to increasing efficiency. These factors brought the seventy-year era of steadily falling electricity generation costs and declining real electricity prices to an abrupt halt. The result, in turn, has been a tremendous upward pressure on electricity rates, primarily because the production of electricity requires large inputs of energy and capital. That is, unlike many of America's basic industries like autos and steel that are relatively more labor-intensive, the electric utility industry is highly capital- and energy-intensive. Its energy and capital costs alone account for roughly 75 percent of the price tag on electricity production.[12] Indeed, the utility industry uses roughly 20 percent of all energy consumed in the United States and accounts for one-fifth of the nation's total invested capital.

Despite these tremendous upward inflationary pressures on electricity prices, for a variety of political, institutional, and ideological reasons that are explored in detail in Chapter 8, the PUCs have been unable, and in some cases simply unwilling, to raise electricity prices fast enough to match the steep rise in energy and capital costs.

10. Atomic Industrial Forum.

11. Scott A. Fenn, *America's Electric Utilities* (Washington, D.C.: Investor Responsibility Research Center, 1983), p. 31, and Atomic Industrial Forum, "Licensing, Design, and construction Problems: Priorities for Solution" (Washington, D.C., 1978), Exhibits 1 and 9.

12. *The Future of Electric Power in America* Washington, D.C.: U.S. Department of Energy, Office of Policy, Planning, and Analysis, June 1983), p. ES–11.

For consumers who have seen their electricity bills skyrocket over the past ten years, this statement may sound strange. (Interestingly, the real, or inflation-adjusted, price of electricity in 1980 was no higher than the price in 1960.)[13] But the fact is that while nominal electricity prices have risen more than 300 percent over the past ten years, energy and capital costs have risen even faster.[14] Thus, despite their dramatic rise, electricity prices have not reflected the utility industry's true market cost of providing power.

As a result of this lagging of regulated electricity prices behind market energy and capital costs of the past decade, the electric utility industry has consistently *failed* its capital-attraction test. In other words, it has been earning a rate of return well below its market cost of capital. According to economists Eugene Brigham and Dilip Shome, the industry's real (inflation-adjusted) earnings have been cut almost in half, to roughly three percentage points below the industry's market cost of equity capital.[15] Economist Howard E. Thompson has found similar evidence of rate suppression; he estimates that utility earnings in the postembargo period have been 40 percent too low.[16]

This failure of the PUCs to set electricity prices that keep pace with inflation has thus far been a windfall to consumers, for the earnings shortfall of the utility is, at least in the short run, a direct gain to consumers.[17] However, such rate suppression has been a disaster to the utility industry, which has seen its financial health deteriorate dramatically. This financial deterioration is evident in several of the industry's financial vital signs.

For example, during the 1960s and early 1970s, electric utilities typically attained bond ratings of AAA and AA—Wall Street's most creditworthy categories. But today, as Figure 1-1 illustrates, many utilities have fallen into the quicksand of BBB and even lower ratings, indicating that they have become highly risky investments. In fact, in every year but one since 1973, more utility bonds have been downgraded than upgraded. These depressed bond ratings can increase a

---

13. Ibid., p. ES-4.

14. Scott A. Fenn, *America's Electric Utilities* (Washington, D.C.: Investor Responsibility Research Center, 1983), p. 24.

15. "Equity Risk Premiums in the 1980s" (University of Florida, 1982). (Working paper no. 58.)

16. "Estimating Return Deficiencies of Electric Utilities 1963-81" (University of Wisconsin, August 1983). (Working paper.)

17. As we shall see in Chapter 7, over time rate suppression typically costs consumers far more than it saves them.

Figure 1–1. Utility Bond Ratings in 1970 and 1982.

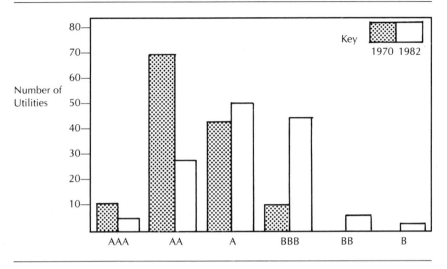

Source: Standard & Poor's Bond Guide.
Note: 130 utilities were rated in 1970; 127 were rated in 1982.

Figure 1–2. Utility Companies' Market-to-Book Ratios, 1962–82.

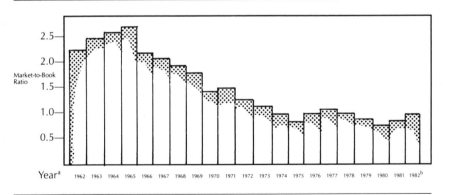

[a]Average of high and low value for the year.
[b]August 1982.
Source: Utility Compustat.

utility's capital costs by several percentage points. The interest rate differential between a AAA-rated and a BBB-rated bond ranges from 100 to 200 basis points; this amounts to an increase in annual interest charges of $10 million to $20 million on a $1-billion bond sale.

Moreover, low bond ratings reduce the pool of potential investors because federal law prohibits certain large institutional investors (from which the bulk of utility capital comes) from buying bonds rated BBB or below.[18]

The electric utilities' fall from financial grace is likewise evident in an equally substantial and prolonged drop in the industry's "market-to-book" ratio. This M/B ratio is simply the ratio of a utility's common stock to the book value of its assets. Figure 1-2 charts its downward trend, which began in the mid 1960s. As the M/B ratio has fallen, so too has the real value of a utility shareholder's common stock. The fact that the ratio has been sinking thus signals the underlying distributional struggle going on in the regulatory arena between utility shareholders and electricity consumers, because in a very real sense, this loss in stock value to shareholders represents a direct gain to ratepayers via PUC rate suppression. That is, the shareholders' loss of stock value is reflected in and caused by lower consumer rates.

Note, however, that this transfer of income is very subtle—a fact that greatly complicates the politics of PUC regulation. Because electricity rates have been steadily rising, increasingly angry ratepayers have come to believe that their utilities are gouging them. But at the same time—and to the distress of investors—the value of utility stocks and bonds has declined because electricity rates are not rising fast enough to meet even more rapidly escalating energy and capital costs.

Despite these redistributional consequences, rate suppression is not simply a "zero-sum game" in which what shareholders lose, ratepayers gain. Indeed, as this book illustrates, rate suppression is a "negative-sum game" in which everyone—shareholders, consumers, and the nation—eventually loses. The reason is that rate suppression fundamentally alters the investment and operating strategies of electric utility executives in such a way as to force these executives to forgo otherwise economic investments necessary to keep the lights on and to keep rates down over time. It is this effect of rate suppression on utility behavior that we explore in the next chapter.

18. The Employment Retirement Income and Securities Act specifies that institutional investors must adhere to the "prudent man" rule, which is generally understood to mean that investment in bonds rated BBB or lower is prohibited.

2 UTILITY CAPITAL MINIMIZATION

The next step in understanding why the dimming of America looms in our electricity future lies in establishing a behavioral link between regulatory rate suppression and the "strategy of capital minimization" that electric utility executives are now pursuing. The essence of this strategy is a systematic underinvestment in new power plants necessary to meet increasing demand and in otherwise economic projects ranging from coal conversion to conservation programs necessary to keep our electricity bills down over time. Studies conducted both by and for the Department of Energy predict that if this systematic capital minimization trend continues, by the year 2000 America will be paying dramatically higher electricity rates for less reliable service.[1] (These effects are the subject of Chapters 5 and 7.)

Understanding how rate suppression has fostered this strategy of capital minimization requires making an important distinction between the short- and the long-term effects of rate suppression. It also requires a brief discussion of an important economic theory—the "Averch-Johnson effect"—propounded in the 1960s by economists Harvey Averch and Leland Johnson.

1. See, for example, *The Future of Electric Power in America* (Washington, D.C.: U.S. Department of Energy, Office of Policy, Planning and Analysis, June 1983), and Peter Navarro, "Long Term Consumer Impacts of Electricity Rate Regulatory Policies" (paper prepared for U.S. Department of Energy, January 1983).

In electric utility regulation, the "short term" is equivalent to the time it takes for a PUC to process a utility's request for a rate increase. In this short time period, the decision a PUC renders in a rate case is, quite literally, a zero-sum transfer in which every dollar of rate relief that the PUC grants to the utility represents a dollar more consumers will have to pay for electricity, and vice versa.

PUC ratemaking is not, however, a zero-sum game, because in the real world neither the regulatory process nor the utility industry itself operates merely in the freeze-frame of a single rate case. Instead, ratemaking occurs over time in a series of rate cases, and utility executives formulate their investment strategies (e.g., how many plants to build) on the basis of the regulatory treatment they expect to receive over the long run. If that regulatory treatment is expected to be favorable, executives are much more likely to risk investing their companies' capital than if such treatment is expected to be rate suppressive.

In the 1960s, economists Averch and Johnson formalized the relationship between regulatory treatment and utility investment strategy in their famous "Averch/Johnson effect."[2] At that time, they predicted that if a utility is allowed to earn a return *higher* than its market cost of capital, it will *overinvest* in new capacity. The logic behind the so-called AJ effect and resultant "goldplating" is that such a generous rate of return provides an incentive for the utility to increase its use of capital, so it tends to build more capacity than it needs to provide service at least cost to consumers. A utility might, for instance, build a power plant it did not really need to meet customer demand simply as a means of boosting profits.

The AJ effect was relevant during the 1960s because technological advances were making it possible for utilities to realize increasing economies of scale, inflation and energy prices were low and stable, and environmental and safety regulations imposed few costs. To at least some observers, the predictions of Averch and Johnson seemed to be borne out when, during the 1960s, some utilities earned more than their regulators intended and power plant construction boomed.[3]

Interestingly, the academic literature of that time failed to explore

2. See Harvey Averch and Leland Johnson, "Behavior of the Firm under Regulatory Constraint," *American Economic Review* (December 1962): 1052.

3. See, for example, R.H. Litzenberger and C.U. Rao, "Estimates of the Marginal Rate of Time Preference and Average Risk Aversion of Investors in Electric Utility Shares 1960–1966" *Bell Journal of Economics* (Spring 1971): 265.

what would happen if a utility earned a return *lower* than its market cost of capital. At that time, it was assumed that any utility in such a losing position would simply withdraw from the market. But today that assumption is generally recognized as flawed, because utilities are legally obligated to continue providing service to consumers, even if it means operating at a loss to investors. Equally important, it is infeasible for a utility to leave its market and use its capital to set up shop elsewhere because that capital is already "sunk"—that is, it exists in the form of large power plants that have few alternative uses.

Today the question of how a utility will respond to inadequate earnings has great relevance because rate suppression is, by definition, a reversal of the conditions that created the original power plant construction boom.

THE REVERSE AJ EFFECT AND CAPITAL MINIMIZATION

After a decade of rate suppression, the utility industry has given us its answer to the question of what investment strategies will result from inadequate returns: *In response to consistently earning less than the market cost of their capital, a large number of utility executives have put the AJ effect in reverse.* Today we are witnessing a dramatic *underinvestment* in new power plants and conversion and conservation projects. In other words, more and more utility executives have adopted a strategy of capital minimization in order to reduce their companies' losses from rate suppression.

Given the remarkable deterioration in the quality and real value of the utility industry's stocks and bonds (as discussed in the previous chapter), this strategy makes perfect economic sense for the utilities— even if it creates what we shall see in Chapters 6 and 7 are substantial economic costs for consumers and the nation. Bluntly stated, the thought behind capital minimization is this: Why should a utility executive spend even one dollar of the firm's capital when he or she expects that the PUC will deny the company the opportunity to earn back a fair market return on that dollar?

Consider the case of issuing common stock to finance, say, the construction of a new power plant. Issuing such stock in the presence of rate suppression virtually guarantees that existing shareholders' stock will be devalued or, as they say on Wall Street, "diluted."[4] This was the lesson utility executives learned in the 1970s when they tried to continue the steady capital expansion of previous decades in the face of declining returns. The falling market-to-book ratios mentioned in Chapter 1 vividly illustrate the poor result.

Similarly, if a utility issues bonds to help finance new construction, rate suppression makes it more difficult for the utility to pay the interest on that debt. Because both profits and cash flow are lower under rate suppression, the funds available to service debt are lower too. The increased risk of default, in turn, is reflected in downward pressure on the utility's bond ratings, in higher capital costs, and in greater difficulty attracting investors to buy the bonds. The easiest way for the executive to prevent such a situation is to avoid investing in new projects. It is often more convenient—indeed more prudent—not to risk exposing the firm to financial default by undertaking such investment. In a nutshell, then, utility executives have adopted a strategy of capital minimization because, in terms of protecting the value of their shareholders' stock and maintaining the financial viability of the firm, such a strategy is sensible.

Evidence of such a strategy abounds. It is found in the widespread delays and cancellations of new power plants, in the refusal and inability of many utilities to aggressively undertake economic petroleum-saving projects such as coal conversion and conservation, in the new willingness of utility executives to rely on purchased power rather than building their own plants, and in a variety of third-party financing schemes that take the onus of new sources of electricity supply off the back of the utility industry—but often at a high cost to consumers.

DELAYS AND CANCELLATIONS

The richest source of evidence of the utilities' strategy of capital minimization is the industry's recent history, which is marked by widespread construction delays and cancellations of new power plants. Today many utility executives who once proclaimed the need for an ambitious program of new power plant construction to meet anticipated

---

4. This dilution occurs because the price of a share of stock is in large part predicated on the return that the stock is expected to proide. If new shares are issued and the return is below that expected return, part of the loss is shared by existing stockholders in the form of falling stock prices (and a falling M/B ratio).

growth in electricity demand have been quietly and systematically delaying or canceling their construction projects.

For example, the North American Electric Reliability Council (NERC) reports that in 1979 over half of the new coal and nuclear capacity scheduled for 1979 through 1988 was delayed an average of almost twenty months.[5] During 1980 alone, utilities canceled or delayed more than half the new capacity they had planned to complete by 1989. In 1981 and 1982, U.S. utilities canceled forty seven major power plant projects that would have boosted capacity by 50 million kilowatts, or 8 percent.[6] From 1977 to 1982 about 140 generating units representing some 150,000 megawatts of electricity were canceled or deferred indefinitely.[7] Further, no new nuclear units have been ordered since 1978, no new orders for *any* major generating projects were placed in 1982,[8] and only one such order was placed in 1983. That order, placed with Westinghouse Electric, was for two 572-megawatt coal units for Southwestern Public Service of Texas's planned generating station near Lubbock, Texas. But "sources at both General Electric and Westinghouse said their companies currently have no assurances for orders in 1984."[9]

Some utility executives have justified these delays and cancellations on the grounds that low economic growth and energy conservation by ratepayers have reduced or eliminated the need for such plants. In fact, there is a good bit of truth in these pronouncements. In the presence of slower economic growth and conservation, the projected growth in electricity demand has slipped from the robust 7 percent annual rate experienced in the 1960s to more modest estimates nearer the current rate of 3 percent.[10] Plants that originally were planned to meet the higher growth rate have legitimately been put on the shelf.

Many of the cancellations and delays, however, speak to a different rationale. For example, Charles J. Dougherty, chief executive officer of Union Electric of St. Louis, explained his company's decision to

5. U.S. Department of Energy, Office of Policy, Planning and Analysis, "The Nation's Electric Future: Perspectives on the Issue of Electricity Supply Sufficiency" (Washington, D.C., February 1982): 15.

6. "The Vicious Circle That Utilities Can't Seem to Break," *Business Week* (May 23, 1983): 178.

7. Atomic Industrial Forum, "Historical Profile of U.S. Nuclear Power Development" (December 31, 1980, updated through November 3, 1982).

8. Scott A. Fenn, *America's Electric Utilities* (Washington, D.C.: Investor Responsibility Research Center, 1983).

9. *Electric Utility Week* (December 26, 1983): 4.

10. U.S. Department of Energy, "The Nation's Electric Future", p. 7.

cancel the second unit of its Callaway nuclear plant, which had been planned to be 1,150 megawatts, by saying that inadequate regulation made funding the unit "very unattractive in spite of the overall economic advantage."[11] Duke Power Company delayed indefinitely completion of its 1,280 megawatt Cherokee Nuclear Station because, in the words of William H. Grigg, the company's legal and financial vice president, "To willingly embark upon a plan to further dilute shareholders' equity by raising new equity through the sale of common stock at below book value would in our view be unconscionable."[12]

Similarly, Justin Moore, chief executive officer of Virginia Electric Power Company, recently canceled a $2 billion nuclear plant on the grounds that, despite its favorable economics, his company simply could not afford to build it.[13] Lelan F. Sillin, Jr. repeatedly announced during his tenure as CEO of Northeast Utilities that until Northeast earned a fair rate of return on new investment, he would not sell new stock to finance either the completion of Millstone 3 (a 1,200-megawatt nuclear unit) or a number of coal-conversion projects—a refusal that led to a long delay in the completion of Millstone 3.[14]

In considering this pattern of delays and cancellations, it is important to remember that capital minimization is not the same as zero capital spending. Indeed, if a utility's plant is more than one-third to one-half completed, it is in the financial interests of that utility to complete the plant as quickly as possible so it can begin earning a return on its investment. A case in point is Commonwealth Edison of Illinois, which is in the midst of completing the construction of five nuclear units that it plans to bring on line by the latter half of the decade.

In such instances, the behavior is again rational because the loss incurred by completing the plant, even under rate suppression, will be less than the loss of simply canceling the plant and forgoing any opportunity to earn a return on the money already invested. In such cases, when progress on the plant is slow, the delays that we observe are due not to the utility executives' unwillingness to fund the project but rather to their firms' financial constraints. Put simply, under rate suppression a utility may be unable—because of low profits and low

11. Statement to the Press, October 9, 1981.

12. Testimony before the South Carolina Public Service Commission, docket no. 80–378–E, August 1981.

13. Peter Navarro, "The Electric Utility Executive's Dilemma," *Harvard Business Review* (May/June 1982): 87.

14. Ibid.

bond ratings—to finance the timely completion of a project already well underway.

Accordingly, under the strategy of capital minimization, we will still observe the utility industry investing considerable funds to finish ongoing projects, but we are not likely to observe many new plans for plant construction or new plant orders. The statistics, some of which were cited earlier, bear this out. According to the Department of Energy, the pattern of plant cancellations conforms well to this predicted profile. That is, industry plant cancellations are either of projects with less than a third of investment already made or of projects that never make it off the drawing board or through the licensing process. Projects more than two-thirds complete are generally being finished.[15]

The fact that the utility industry has virtually halted new orders on major generating projects further confirms the theory. If present patterns continue, there may not be enough economic power plants to meet electricity demand in some regions of the country and, because of the long eight-to twelve-year construction periods, there won't be time to build them when the shortages begin. A 1983 report by the Department of Energy predicted that even if electricity demand growth was very slow, by the 1990s supply would not meet demand in some regions and unreliable electric service might be experienced in such areas as Texas, Kansas, Arkansas, Louisiana, and parts of the midwest, unless utilities revised their existing construction plans upward.[16]

In considering this dramatic slowdown in new plant construction, it should also be pointed out that a strategy of capital minimization slows *all* types of utility investment. Thus, while the bulk of delays and cancellations necessitated by budget cuts have been of larger, central-station coal or nuclear plants, a strategy of capital minimization also discourages new investment in a wide variety of alternative sources of electricity supply, such as wind, solar, geothermal, and biomass.

COAL CONVERSIONS AND CONSERVATION

Plant delays and cancellations are only the tip of the capital minimiza-

15. "Pulling the Nuclear Plug," *Time*, February 13, 1984, p. 34.
16. *The Future of Electric Power in America: Economic Supply for Economic Growth*, (Washington, DC: U.S. Department of Energy, Office of Policy, Planning, and Analysis, June 1983): 4-1 through 4-40.

tion iceberg, however. As we shall discuss in more detail in the next chapter, there are more than a hundred large power plants, located primarily in California and in the Northeast, that now burn oil but that could economically be converted to coal.[17] At the same time, many baseload plants in the Gulf Coast region could switch from natural gas to coal and, in so doing, save customers millions of dollars as natural gas is continually and gradually deregulated.

However, since the 1973–74 series of OPEC price increases that first made some of the conversion projects economic and even after the second quantum jump in oil prices in 1979, only about one-third of the economic conversions have taken place.[18] Besides a variety of environmental-regulation difficulties and permit problems, the financial inability and, in many cases, the unwillingness of utility executives to finance such multimillion-dollar projects in the face of rate suppression have held back these economic conversions.

Similarly, many utilities have failed to pursue energy conservation to the extent possible, despite the wisdom of energy economists that it is often cheaper to save a barrel of oil than it is to burn one.[19] (Hereafter, the term *conservation* will include load management techniques, which are designed to reduce periods of peak demand and thus eliminate the need for some new capacity.) Reluctance to undertake conservation programs is, again, based on the fact that although they require considerably less investment than new power plants, such programs still cost money. That point is often lost on consumer advocates who preach conservation as *the* solution to the electricity problem and who fail to recognize that the bulk of conservation to date has been by electricity users rather than by the utilities themselves.

The fact that utility conservation does indeed require considerable investment is attested to by the capital budgets of several utilities that have actually undertaken aggressive conservation programs. In Oregon, Montana, Washington, Idaho, and northern California, Pacific Powerer & Light spent $37 million on weatherization and home energy audits from 1978 through 1983.[20] Similarly, Pacific Gas & Electric has approved a zero-interest loan program for the installation of insulation,

---

17. *Staff Analysis of the Energy and Economic Impacts of the President's Program for Reducing Oil and Gas Consumption in the Utility Sector*, (Washington, D.C.: U.S. Department of Energy, Office of Electrical Systems, Policy and Evaluation, April 21, 1980).

18. Department of Energy spokesperson.

19. This was a point popularized by *Energy Future*, Daniel Yergin and Robert Stobaugh, ed. (New York: Random House, 1980).

20. Pacific Power & Light Spokesperson.

weather-stripping, and other conservation devices and has slated $115 million for these activities, while the Environmental Defense Fund has testified that a $1.5 billion investment in conservation would save 32,300 gigawatt hours per year of electricity generation in California.[21]

THIRD-PARTY FINANCING AND PURCHASED POWER

Finally, evidence of the utility industry's strategy of capital minimization may be found in a growing trend toward electricity supply projects financed by various third parties. Such third-party transactions include the purchasing of power from Canada and Mexico as well as from domestic cogenerators.

In the case of foreign purchases, utilities are able to forgo making capital investments by entering into contracts with Canada or Mexico for the power needed to meet growing demand or to replace some of their more expensive existing oil- or gas-fired capacity. In effect, Mexico and Canada build the plants that America otherwise would have to.

In 1982 America imported more than 34 billion kilowatt hours from Canada at a cost of $835 million, and that figure may double by 1985.[22] At the same time, roughly 8,000 megawatt hours of Mexican power crossed into the United States, and a variety of utilities are currently negotiating to raise these imports substantially over the coming decades.[23]

In an open, global economy where there are substantial benefits to be gained from free trade, there is nothing inherently wrong with such foreign purchases. Aside from the questions of reliability and national security that these purchases raise, it can be quite economic for the United States to buy rather than generate its power. For example, the state of New York currently receives over 12 percent of its electricity from Canada, and under current contracts much if perhaps not all of this power helps to substantially reduce New York consumers' electricity bills.[24]

21. Pacific Gas & Electric information office, and testimony of W.R.Z. Willey, Staff Economist, Environmental Defense Fund, Inc., before the California Public Utilities Commission, Application nos. 57284, 57285, 1978, "Alternative Energy Systems for Pacific Gas & Electric Co.: An Economic Analysis."
22. Staff report, Economic Regulatory Administration.
23. For example, San Diego Gas and Electric is currently building the Southwest Power Link, which would connect its customers to geothermal power producers in Mexico.
24. "The Vicious Circle That Utilities Can't Seem to Break," p. 178.

In some circumstances, however, reliance on purchased power can create a costly problem for electricity consumers. The problem arises when the price a utility pays for such purchased power is higher than the cost the utility would incur if it were to build its own plants to supply the power instead. Rate suppression makes such a situation probable because as part of its strategy of capital minimization a utility may well opt to buy rather than build. This is so because in the "build" scenario the utility's shareholders lose, via rate suppression; in the "buy" scenario it is consumers who lose, but that loss is less obvious.

A case in point is offered by Boston Edison. The management of Edison recently canceled plans to complete its 1,150 megawatt Pilgrim 2 nuclear facility. That plant was originally intended to replace some of Edison's more expensive oil-fired capacity during the late 1980s and then to meet increased electricity demand in the 1990s. Since Pilgrim 2's cancellation, Edison has opted to buy Canadian power to fill its needs.

What is most interesting about this purchase agreement is the public relations campaign Boston Edison used to justify it. The primary message of the campaign was that Canadian power would save Edison's ratepayers 20 percent on their bills. As far as Edison's story went, this was in fact true because Edison's Canadian contract effectively set the price of the purchased power at roughly 80 percent of what it would cost Edison's own oil-fired plants to produce it.

However, the campaign neglected to say that the completion of Pilgrim 2 (rather than its cancellation) would likely have saved Edison ratepayers even more; according to Edison's calculations, right up until the cancellation of the Pilgrim 2 unit, this nuclear facility would have been cheaper over the life of the plant than Edison's existing oil capacity and any new coal-powered generating unit.[25] Pilgrim 2 would also have been cheaper in the long run than Canadian power.[26] But because of "regulatory uncertainties"—not the least of which was the expectation of rate suppression by the Massachusetts PUC—Edison's management chose to explore the safer path of third-party

25. Ed Selgrade, former Massachusetts DPU commissioner.

26. Pilgrim 2 would likely have come on line in 1986 or 1987. Over the period 1987–1994, the cost of Pilgrim 2 would have been greater than the cost of purchasing Canadian power under the ten-year contract signed in 1984. But if Boston Edison enters into a 30-year purchase agreement, then Pilgrim 2 would have been less expensive.

purchases, which promised to be less costly at least in the short run and less risky to investors.[27]

The utility industry's increasing reliance on cogeneration likewise illustrates that what is in some cases a good thing may in other cases be a bad one. Cogeneration refers to the production of heat and electrical energy from the same primary energy source. Cogenerated electricity is most often produced by process manufacturers, such as for paper products, chemicals, and primary metals. Manufacturers that use high-temperature steam or direct heat generally use only part of their heat-producing capacity. By investing in a high-pressure boiler and a turbine generator set, they can burn more fuel to produce steam at high enough pressure to produce electricity.

Cogeneration is an old practice that dates back to the late 1880s. Between that time and the early 1900s, electricity generation at industrial sites was fairly common. As electricity service was extended and prices fell, however, industry gradually stopped producing its own electrical power. Today there is a resurgence of interest in cogeneration.

For the pulp and paper and steel industries, cogeneration is not only an efficient and economical way to produce electricity but also a convenient way of disposing of by-products. The pulp and paper industry has large amounts of burnable wastes that can be used to fuel cogenerators, and the steel industry gives off gases from open hearths that can be used as fuel to produce steam.

Despite its sound economics under some circumstances, cogeneration doesn't always make sense, particularly under the federal law that was designed to establish for cogenerators both a market for their power and a favorable price. This law, the Public Utility Regulatory Policy Act of 1978 (PURPA), establishes a cogeneration market by requiring electric utilities to purchase all the power that is generated by qualified cogenerators. At the same time, PURPA establishes a favorable price for cogenerators by requiring utilities to pay them their "avoided cost." That is, the utility must pay the cogenerator a price equal to what it would have cost the utility to produce that power with its existing plant.

For most utilities, this avoided-cost doctrine means that they must pay cogenerators a price equivalent to their most expensive source of

27. For details of this incident, see Peter Navarro and Thomas R. Stauffer, "The Public May Be the Big Loser in Pilgrim Power-Plant Cancellation," *Boston Globe* (October 14, 1981).

generation, which is usually the oil-fired or gas-fired plant that is in line for displacement. This requirement severely limits a utility's ability to bargain with a cogenerator for a good price for its customers. Some utilities, such as Granite State Electric Company in New Hampshire, Pacific Gas & Electric, San Diego Gas & Electric, and Southern California Edison, have challenged this interpretation.

Reliance on third-party cogenerators, of course, fits neatly into the utility industry's strategy of capital minimization. It saves them from building new plants. However, it is easy to see how PURPA can wind up costing consumers more money. For one thing, the avoided-cost pricing mechanism is tied not to the cogenerators' costs but rather to the high end of the utility's costs. This means that even if a cogenerator can provide power at two to three cents a kilowatt hour, the utility may be forced to pay more than double that amount.

More important, however, the avoided-cost doctrine typically has not allowed avoided cost to be calculated on the basis of possible new power plant construction. The price of cogenerated power is tied only to the price of electricity produced from *existing* plants, which is often more expensive than that from new replacements. If the avoided-cost doctrine were based on the cost of producing power via new plants, the price of cogenerated power could be much less to consumers. In such a case, two good things could happen at the same time.

First, the low avoided-cost price might eliminate some inefficient cogenerators from the market. In their stead, the utility would build its own cheaper capacity; then rates would be lower and the nation's allocation of energy and capital resources would be improved. Second, efficient cogenerators might supply some power at a lower profit, and rates to consumers would drop accordingly.

Because of rate suppression, the utility industry is willing to go along with the cogeneration situation to avoid the need to undertake capital investment. But because of PURPA, uneconomic cogeneration is encouraged and thus creates upward pressure on consumers' electricity bills.

In summary, we have seen that regulatory rate suppression induces utility executives to pursue a strategy of capital minimization; the logic of this rate-suppression/capital-minimization syndrome is embodied in the reverse Averch/Johnson effect. In a reverse-AJ world, capital minimization is merely a second-best means for a utility to meet its regulatory mandate while ensuring its survival.

This behavioral response manifests itself through widespread delays and cancellations of new power plants and a dearth of new plans for such plants; a continual failure to achieve the substantial economic gains available from investments in both coal conversion and conservation; and an increased reliance on purchasing power from third-party foreign suppliers in Canada and Mexico and domestic cogenerators. In Part II, we examine three regulatory penalties created by the effect of rate suppression on utility investment, an effect hereafter referred to as the rate-suppression/capital-minimization syndrome.

II THREE REGULATORY PENALTIES

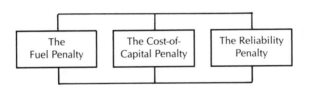

| The Fuel Penalty | The Cost-of-Capital Penalty | The Reliability Penalty |

3 THE FUEL PENALTY

The first regulatory penalty imposed by the rate-suppression/capital-minimization syndrome is the fuel penalty. This penalty equals the savings a utility forgoes when it fails to undertake the capital investment necessary to achieve its most economic generation mix—that is, when it fails to build the mix of power plants that will deliver electricity to consumers at the lowest cost over time. The supply options include coal, hydro, nuclear, solar, geothermal, biomass, and wind plants as well as conservation, which represents a supply option in that it can reduce the need for new capacity.

Each utility's most economic generation mix is unique. The optimal mix depends primarily on the utility's location relative to various energy sources and on the mix of its existing plants (especially how many noneconomic oil and gas plants it relies on).

The most economic generation mix of a utility in the Sunbelt Southwest that is located relatively close to abundant coal reserves, for example, would typically consist primarily of coal-fired power plants and perhaps some solar and wind capacity (although even a utility sitting literally atop a resource like coal may want to diversify its generation mix to avoid overexposure to an incident such as a prolonged coal strike). If that utility currently is using a lot of natural gas to generate electricity, achieving its most economic generation mix would likely also require replacement of those gas plants. While such gas plants were economic before the OPEC price shocks, as a rule they have become economically obsolete because of higher petroleum prices in the postembargo world.

In contrast, the most economic generation mix of a utility in the Frostbelt Northeast, typically will include more nuclear power plants than in the Southwest. If that Northeastern utility also has considerable oil-fired capacity that formerly burned coal, it will likely find it economic in a postembargo world to convert those plants back to coal. (Despite the greater costs of transporting coal from mines to plants, coal is still a cheaper fuel than oil in the Northeast.) At the same time, a Northeastern utility is likely to find investments in conservation more attractive than would other regions of the country where it costs less to generate electricity because of greater proximity to energy sources. Similarly, utilities in the heavily dammed Pacific Northwest will favor relatively more hydro power, California utilities will favor more geothermal power, and so on.

When a utility fails to undertake the capital investment necessary to arrive at its most economic generation mix, its costs of providing power to ratepayers are higher than they otherwise would be. These higher costs represent forgone savings; these forgone savings are referred to here as the fuel penalty, because the largest part of the savings typically consists of potential reductions in a utility's total fuel bill.

Major sources of the fuel penalty include: failure to replace existing noneconomic power plants (typically oil and gas) with new nonpetroleum power plants; failure to pursue to the fullest extent possible economic opportunities for coal conversions and conservation; and reliance on purchased power that is more expensive than potential internally generated electricity (i.e., building one's own plants).

As we saw in Chapter 2, these investments are precisely the ones that utility executives are likely to pass up under rate suppression. These otherwise economic investments might not be undertaken because a utility may be unable to finance them (also a function of rate suppression), community groups may oppose them, and regulatory and permitting delay may halt construction. But a major reason, of course, is that rate suppression makes it "uneconomic" for the utility to undertake these otherwise economic investments by denying the utility its full share of the savings that such investments would provide to utility shareholders and electricity consumers alike. Indeed, instead of saving money for its shareholders, any such investment loses money. In the remainder of this chapter, we examine the sources of this fuel penalty and in doing so come to understand its magnitude, which runs into billions of dollars.

NEW POWER PLANTS TO DISPLACE OIL AND GAS CAPACITY

When oil cost one or two dollars per barrel and natural gas cost ten to twenty cents per thousand cubic foot (mcf), as in the 1950s and 1960s, it made perfect economic sense for the utility industry to build substantial oil and gas capacity to meet an electricity demand that was growing at an annual rate of 7 percent. Because it did precisely that, the utility industry is now the single largest stationary consumer of petroleum in the nation (the stationary category excludes cars, trucks, and planes).[1] Today, the electric utility industry accounts for roughly 10 percent of the nation's combined oil and natural gas consumption, while more than one-fifth of all electricity generated in the United States comes from petroleum-fired plants.

In the 1970s, the price of oil climbed over 1,000 percent, from the one- and two-dollars-a-barrel range to the ethereal OPEC heights of twenty to thirty dollars a barrel. The price of natural gas in unregulated markets has climbed in lock step with these oil price hikes and now sells in such markets for anywhere from three to seven dollars per mcf. (Since gas is a close substitute for oil as well as a generally superior fuel, its price closely tracks the price of oil over the long term.)

Not surprisingly, many of the petroleum-fired power plants that were built with the expectation of a cheap supply of oil and gas have become uneconomic in the postembargo world. Figure 3–1 illustrates the remarkable difference the rise in oil and gas prices has made on the economics of petroleum-fired power plants. In the figure, the unshaded areas show the average preembargo 1973 price of different types of electricity generating capacity, including coal, nuclear, hydro, oil, and natural gas, while the shaded areas indicate the 1981 postembargo price of such generation.

1. Oil and natural gas are treated as substitutes throughout this book an are referred to as "petroleum." The designation is an important one from the standpoint of national energy policy: Once gas is displaced from under utility boilers, it can serve to displace oil from other sectors—primarily the industrial but also the residential and commercial sectors—thus indirectly reducing oil imports.

Figure 3–1.   Electricity Prices by Primary-Generation Fuel.

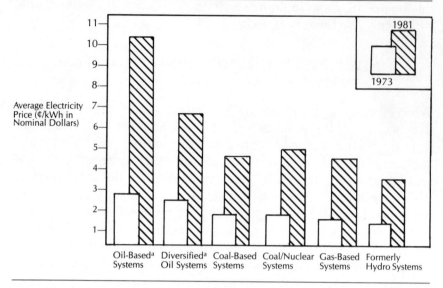

[a]"Oil-based systems" are systems that used oil as a primary-generation fuel through the period. "Diversified oil systems" are systems that substituted a substantial amount of coal and nuclear generation for oil generation over the period.

Source: Booz, Allen & Hamilton Price Disparities Report.

As the figure clearly shows, prior to 1973 the difference between the average price of electricity generated by the major fuel types was slight. By 1981 the cost of oil-fired generation had climbed to more than double that of other systems; if natural gas were totally deregulated (as it will be in 1985), the same disparity in costs would be true for gas plants as well.

The large economic disadvantage that now burdens oil plants (one that natural gas plants will share after deregulation under federal law) illustrates a point crucial to understanding the fuel penalty: At current and projected petroleum prices, it is now cheaper to build, operate, and fuel a new nonpetroleum plant than it is to continue to fuel and operate most petroleum power plants.[2] In fact, the Department of Energy has estimated that it is economic to replace over half of all the

2. For discussion, see Peter Navarro, "The Soft, Hard, or Smart Path: Charting the Electric Utility Industry's Future," *Public Utilities Fortnightly* (June 18, 1981): 25.

large baseload petroleum power plants now operating in the United States.[3]

Thus, while many of today's petroleum power plants are still useful in the sense that they can still produce electricity, these plants have become *economically obsolete*. That is, the nation and electricity consumers would be better off if the utility industry simply put these still-operable plants in mothballs and replaced them with new nonpetroleum plants; the result would be lower electricity prices and fewer imports of foreign oil.

Accordingly, we can distinguish between power plants needed to meet increased electricity demand and those needed for a utility to achieve its most economic generation mix. In the former case, failure to build such plants threatens to dim the lights and leads, as we shall see in Chapter 5, to the reliability penalty. In the latter case, the purpose of new construction is to provide the same level of service to consumers but to do so at a lower price. A failure to do so in this instance means lost savings in the form of the fuel penalty.

Given the tendency of today's utility executives to favor a strategy of capital minimization and considering that over one-half of today's petroleum capacity is economically obsolete, it is easy to deduce that the nation is currently incurring a sizable fuel penalty by failing to build new plants for petroleum displacement. While more precise estimates of this new-construction component of the fuel penalty will be given in the discussion of consumer welfare under rate suppression in Chapter 7, it is worth pointing out that in 1979, the National Electric Reliability Council predicted that delays in the construction of coal and nuclear power plants originally scheduled for 1979 through 1988 threatened to boost the nation's oil consumption by some two billion barrels over that period.[4] This additional oil consumption will not only exacerbate our dependence on foreign imports but will also

3. "Staff Analysis of the Energy and Economic Impacts of the President's Program for Reducing Oil and Gas Consumption in the Utility Sector," (Washington, D.C.: U.S. Department of Energy, Office of Electrical Systems, Policy and Evaluation, April 21, 1981). Note that baseload generating capacity is to be distinguished from intermediate (cycling) capacity and peaking capacity. Baseload plants can be run constantly at high operating rates. These capital-intensive units produce power at high rates of thermal efficiency but require long startup times. Intermediate-load plants are cycled to meet the swings of demand over a wide range of less pronounced daily peaks of electricity demand (e.g., the daily peak that typically occurs around dinnertime). Peaking plants have low capital costs and quick startup times, but because of their low thermal efficiencies and more expensive fuel choice (typically oil or gas), they have high running costs; they are used the equivalent of a few days each year to meet peak demand.

4. U.S. Department of Energy, Office of Policy and Evaluation, "Reducing U.S. Oil Vulnerability," Washington, D.C., p. V–E–34.

boost electricity rates by billions of dollars.

The magnitude of the fuel penalty can be further inferred from the savings some utilities have made by constructing new power plants to replace their oil or gas guzzlers. Take, for example, Northeast Utilities (NU), a Connecticut-based utility that supplies power to both Connecticut and Massachusetts. During the 1970s, it successfully replaced several of its existing oil-fired baseload plants with two new nuclear units, Millstone 1 and 2, totaling 1,520 megawatts. According to NU, the new plants now save consumers over $300 million per year and reduce the nation's annual oil consumption by 18 million barrels a year.[5] Similarly, Baltimore Gas and Electric Company's Calvert Cliffs nuclear plant saves its customers over $2 million in oil costs each year.[6]

COAL CONVERSIONS

In any discussion of building new nonpetroleum power plants to replace oil and gas capacity, a question inevitably arises: Why not just switch or convert existing petroleum plants to the most logical substitute, coal, rather than simply mothballing them, as premature retirement seems to imply? The answer to that question hinges on a very basic conversion rule: In general, unless a petroleum plant was originally built to burn coal, it will be uneconomic to convert that plant to coal. The primary reason is that petroleum-fired boilers are smaller than coal-fired ones, so that any conversion would require a major modification and possibly total replacement of one of the most expensive parts of the plant. In most cases, it is more sensible to build a new plant, especially if the existing oil or gas plant has already seen over half its service life. Another obstacle to conversion is that oil- and gas-fired plants, which don't use large stockpiles for their fuel supply, often lack storage facilities for a bulky fuel like coal, so that even if it is possible and economic to convert the boiler, space constraints may rule out converting the plant.

While the conversion rule often makes new power plant construction for replacement purposes sensible, a large number of power plants do pass the conversion test. At last count more than 100 large petroleum-fired plants that formerly burned coal could economically be converted back to that fuel.[7]

5. Northeast Utilities research department.
6. Baltimore Gas & Electric information office.
7. Peter Navarro, "Electric Utility Regulation and National Energy Policy," *Regulation* (January/February 1981): 20.

Figure 3–2. Comparison of Levelized Costs of a New Coal-Fired Power Plant in 1990 with an Existing Oil-Fired Facility (in mid-1982 dollars).

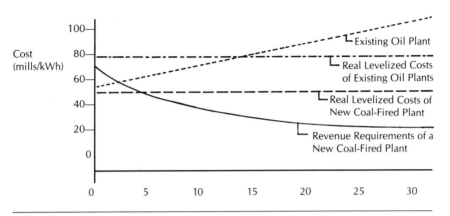

Source: *The Future of Electric Power in America* (Washington, D.C.: U.S. Department of Energy, June 1983).

Most of these coal-capable plants are located in the Northeast region and in Florida. Ironically, these plants are the product of an earlier shift in national priorities: During the 1960s when the nation was first trying to clean up its air pollution, many utilities were ordered to convert or voluntarily converted their plants to the then low-priced petroleum.

Now national priorities have again shifted, and it has become both economical and in the interest of national security to switch back to coal. (Figure 3–2 illustrates the superior economics of coal-fired plants.) At the same time, advancements in air pollution technology have made it possible for such conversions to take place without an increase in air pollution and even with possible decreases. According to one estimate, converting these plants would reduce national oil consumption by 400,000 barrels per day, or 146 million barrels per year, while saving ratepayers over $10 million a day, or over $3 billion per year.[8] In the oil-dependent Northeast alone, more than 4,000 megawatts of oil capacity could be economically converted to coal.

8. Ibid.

The investment of $1.34 billion would pay $5.2 billion back to New England consumers.[9]

As with the case of new power plant construction to displace petroleum plants, a look at some successful conversions gives us a better grip on the fuel penalty imposed on ratepayers. The New England Electric System (NEES) has been at the forefront of the aggressive pursuit of coal-conversion opportunities. Its first project was a 1,150 megawatt plant at Brayton Point. This project cost a total of $192 million; but according to NEES it now saves ratepayers $110 million a year and the nation 11 million barrels of oil a year.[10]

The Brayton Point project also illustrates how coal conversion can sometimes help reduce air pollution. In the conversion process, NEES installed electrostatic precipitators, and it entered into coal contracts that carefully specified how clean the delivered coal must be. (Brayton Point had formerly been burning a medium-grade sulfur oil.) The result of these pollution control measures is a 20 percent reduction of sulfur dioxide emissions and a 50 percent reduction of particulate emissions.[11] Along with Brayton Point, NEES has also converted three plants at its Salem Harbor facility to realize savings of some $32 million a year and 3 million barrels of oil a year.[12]

A second example is offered by the Virginia Electric & Power Company (VEPCO), which has been converting its oil plants to coal since 1975. According to VEPCO, when its conversion program is complete in 1986 (1.8 million kilowatt hours of a total 2.8 million have already been converted), its ratepayers will have saved roughly $1 billion in fuel costs.[13]

Despite these successes, only one-third of the nation's noneconomic, coal-capable petroleum capacity has been converted.[14] Two-thirds of that capacity—equivalent to almost 500,000 barrels of petroleum a day—still remain unconverted. Obstacles to conversion include environmental permits, licensing, and the like. But a lack of financing capability, together with a lack of willingness on the part of most

---

9. *The Economics of Coal Conversion* (Washington, D.C.: U.S. Department of Energy, October 1981). (Prepared by Mitnick & Associates, Inc.)

10. New England Electric Systems research department.

11. Ibid.

12. Ibid.

13. Virginia Electric & Power Company 1981 Corporate Report, Richmon, Va.

14. Peter Navarro, "The Soft, Hard, or Smart Path: Charting the Electric Utility Industry's Future," *Public Utilities Fortnightly* (June 18, 1981): 25.

utility executives, remains the major obstacle to realizing the potential savings of conversions.

CONSERVATION

To paraphrase an old adage, "a barrel of oil saved is a barrel of oil earned." This important point underlies the claims made by numerous advocates of conservation and in a range of books including *Energy Future* and *Soft Energy Paths* that the best way to beat our oil import problem is simply to stop using so much of it.[15]

There is much truth in this adage. After 1973, electricity intensity (the amount of electricity used divided by the size of the economy) leveled off, largely because of price-induced conservation. Had the trend of electricity intensity of earlier decades continued, the United States would have needed as much as 127,000 megawatts of additional capacity in 1981.[16] A wide range of conservation options can reduce not only oil consumption but total energy use as well. These options range from simple measures like home insulation, storm windows, and caulking to more sophisticated methods such as the installation of individual meters, peak load switches, electrothermal storage devices, and heat pumps.

In examining the conservation option and its impact on the fuel penalty, three points must be considered. The first is that, like anything, conservation has its limits. While there are many investments that utilities and consumers can now make that would save money by cutting fuel and electricity bills, there is a point of diminishing returns at which the logic of "it costs less to save a barrel of oil than to burn one" reverses itself.

For example, a homeowner might find that a $2,000 investment in roof insulation might cut his or her electricity heating bill by $1,000 per year for ten years. With a two-year payback and eight years of pure savings, such an investment would be clearly economic. However, after exhausting most of the more economic conservation options (storm windows, storm doors, and the like) another $2,000 investment

---

15. Daniel Yergin and Robert Stobaugh, ed., *Energy Future* (New York: Random House, 1979); and Amory B. Lovins, *Soft Energy Paths* (Cambridge, Mass.: Ballinger, 1977), also published by Friends of the Earth.

16. *The Future of Electric Power in America* (Washington, D.C.: U.S. Department of Energy, Office of Policy, Planning, and Analysis, June 1983), p. 5-50.

in conservation for, say, wall insulation might cut the heating bill only another $180 per year for ten years. Such a small annual savings wouldn't even pay back the original investment. It would be cheaper to use the electricity than to try to save it.

The second point for consideration is that evidence suggests that neither the utility industry nor its consumers have reached that point of negative return on conservation investment. Accordingly, there is economic opportunity for the industry to embrace the conservation option more fully than it has.

At the utility-specific level, the Environmental Defense Fund (EDF) has argued that improved end-use efficiencies (via retrofitting and stricter appliance and building standards) would allow Pacific Gas & Electric Company to achieve a reduction in electricity demand of some 32,300 gigawatt hours a year.[17] By combining conservation with exploitation of potential cogeneration, geothermal, and wind capacity, PG&E could reduce oil-fired capacity by 1,282 gigawatt hours by 1996.

This brings us to a third and final point: Although conservation can cost less than the new power plant it makes unnecessary, it, like new power plant construction and coal conversion, still requires substantial investment. For example, according to a study conducted by the Alliance to Save Energy, the $89 million present value savings to be passed on to Arkansas Power & Light ratepayers by 1988 requires an $86 million investment in conservation.[18] That conservation program would reduce demand by 34 megawatts by 1988 at a cost of $650 per kilowatt hour, which is less than the roughly $950 per kilowatt hour a new plant would require but is still a substantial amount of money. Similarly, PG&E would have to spend over some $1.5 billion to follow EDF's soft path to conservation and alternative energy savings.[19]

It is not surprising, then, that in an era of rate suppression we are witnessing a large potential for conservation that is being ignored by capital-minimizing utilities. From the estimates above, it is clear that this conservation component is yet another contributor to a growing fuel penalty.

17. W.R.Z. Willey, staff economist, Environmental Defense Fund, "Alternative Energy Systems for Pacific Gas & Electric Co.: An Economic Analysis" (prepared testimony before the California Public Utilities Commission, 1978), p. A13.
18. "Utility Promotion of Investment in Energy Efficiency: Engineering, Legal, and Economic Analyses, Summary," Alliance to Save Energy (Washington D.C., December 1983), p. 8.
19. Willey, "Alternative Energy Systems for Pacific Gas & Electric."

PURCHASED POWER

When rate suppression reduces the financial capability of, and incentives for, a utility to build new power plants, often the second-best way for the company to meet its projected power needs is to purchase power, either from foreign sources such as Canada or Mexico or from other utilities with surplus capacity. While such purchases can be economical, there are several reasons why purchased power sometimes costs more than self-generated power, thereby constituting the purchased-power component of the fuel penalty.

The most important reason that purchased power may be uneconomic has to do with how contracts for it are negotiated. We have already seen in Chapter 2 how federal law can make cogeneration contracts a bad deal. A close look at two other kinds of contractual arrangements with both foreign and domestic power sellers sheds further light on this component of the fuel penalty.

At present, Canada is our major source of imported electricity; it sends some 34 billion kilowatt hours across its border to feed the lines of the Power Authority of the State of New York (PASNY), Boston Edison, and Minnesota Power & Light, to name just a few.[20] That is as much electricity as would be generated by twelve large coal-fired power plants or six large nuclear plants. For that power, Americans pay almost a billion dollars to Canada each year.

Most of the power that Canada sends us is produced by hydroelectric dams, one of the cheapest ways to generate electricity. In fact, most of the Canadian power costs less than one cent per kilowatt hour to generate (although transmission costs add a bit more to the final price). This compares with a current cost of 3.1 to 2.7 cents for nuclear power, 3.5 to 3.2 cents for coal-fired generation, and 7.0 to 6.9 cents for oil-fired generation.[21]

On the surface, then, it would seem that buying Canadian power is a good deal. However, there is a hitch: The cheap Canadian power does not cross our border with a modest markup of, say, 50 to 100 percent. Instead, because of Canadian energy policy, that power is marked up by as much as 500 percent.

According to the National Energy Board of Canada, the contract

20. For yearly figures on Canadian electricity exports, see *World Energy Industry*, Fourth Quarter, 1982, Volume III, Number 1 (San Diego, CA: Business Information Display, 1983), p. 34.

21. Averages from the Atomic Industrial Forum Survey.

price of all power sold to America must be linked not to its generating cost but rather to the price of oil. Thus, when Hydro Quebec negotiated with PASNY, the contract terms required the buyer to pay the oil-generating equivalent, less adjustments for transmission costs and a small discount. The final price works out to be about 80 percent of the cost of generating the power using a petroleum plant, or more than a nickel per kilowatt hour.

For PASNY, this may—or may not—be a good deal. It now pays roughly a nickel per kilowatt hour for power that costs less than one cent for Canada to generate. While that nickel is cheaper than the cost of oil-fired generation that would have to be used in lieu of Canadian power (7.5 cents per kilowatt hour on average), it is certainly *not* cheaper than the price New Yorkers pay for power generated by several nuclear units in the state. For example, the four New York nuclear plants that have come on line since 1970 produce electricity at an average of 3.7 cents per kilowatt hour.[22] Nor is PASNY's nickel power cheaper than coal; in 1982, coal-fired units produced electricity at an average cost of 3.1 cents per kilowatt hour.[23]

It is clear that if PASNY had instead arranged ten years ago for the construction of a new coal unit to furnish the power the Canadians are now supplying, its ratepayers would be paying not only less than its equivalent oil-generated costs but also less than the "Canadian bargain." Moreover, even if PASNY now arranged for a new coal unit to replace the Canadian connection, the projected on-line costs of such plants would be less than the nickel per kilowatt hour. (Cost estimates for a coal unit entering service in 1995—which assumes construction starts now—are 4.3 cents.)[24]

Canada's pricing policy—in concert with the rate-suppression/capital-minimization syndrome—has, then, a very clear potential for penalizing American ratepayers. That penalty is the price we pay for Canadian power minus the price we would have paid for our own domestically generated power. Even if the savings were a mere one cent, they would amount to roughly $340 million annually for current power purchases and roughly double that over the next two decades.

Our Canadian cousins are not the only ones to enjoy the benefits of rate suppression at ratepayers' expense. In the United States, there is a

22. Atomic Industrial Forum, Public Affairs Office.
23. Ibid.
24. National Energy Information Center.

different kind of income redistribution among the ratepayers and shareholders of utilities that buy and sell electricity to other U.S. utilities. At present, over 10 percent of the power generated in the United States is sold in the bulk power market.[25]

As with foreign purchases, these domestic power transfers are not necessarily bad. In fact, many of these purchases are quite sensible and reflect "economic dispatch," a practice designed to minimize electricity costs. The principle behind economic dispatch is that utilities, which typically have joined a power-sharing pool, combine their generating capacity; depending on the level of demand, the power pool then uses the cheapest plants to generate electricity and allocates supplies among the participants according to need. Thus, in a period of low demand, a utility with expensive petroleum capacity will generate very little of its own electricity and will instead purchase it from another utility in the power pool with more nonpetroleum units. The shared savings from such arrangements amount to billions of dollars each year.

A different kind of purchase that has proliferated during the last decade of rate suppression may not be so beneficial, however, at least to the ratepayers of the buying utilities. Under long-term contracts for power, some utilities have been buying the rights to portions of plants owned by other utilities. In some cases, utilities are making such purchases in lieu of constructing their own plants.

Public Service of Colorado, for example, has shelved its plans to build a number of coal units and instead is purchasing power from a variety of sources, especially the city of Colorado Springs.[26] Similarly, a number of California utilities have scrapped plans to build additional plants and instead are buying, or plan to buy, power that will be transmitted from the coal-rich Southwest power basin: San Diego Gas & Electric Company has contracted to buy some 150 megawatts of power from Tucson Electric Power Company and more than 236 megawatts from Public Service Company of New Mexico, while Southern California Edison has an agreement to buy power from Arizona Public Service Company.

From the standpoint of national energy policy, such purchases may not be bad. In fact, it may make sense for America to regionalize or

---

25. *Projected Costs of Electricity from Nuclear and Coal-fired Power Plants,* Energy Information Administration DOE.EIA-3056/1, August 1982.

26. Public Service of Colorado Public Affairs Office.

cluster its electricity generators in, say, the Southwest, where coal is abundant and population density is low. However, from the standpoint of the ratepayers of these Colorado and California utilities (and other buyers), such purchases often are no bargain. In some cases, the price of the purchased power is set unduly high in the negotiations between the buying and selling utilities. The Southwest utilities, knowing that the buyers are unwilling or unable to build their own plants but will need the power, have had a negotiating advantage. Accordingly, like our Canadian cousins, they have agreed to sell power at prices higher than their own costs and at prices that likely would exceed those of self-generated electricity by the buyers.[27]

Note, then, the winners and losers that rate suppression creates by increasing purchased power: The shareholders of the selling utility gain in the form of high profits from purchases, while the shareholders of the buying utility likewise gain because the purchases reduce the need for capital investment, which would be unprofitable under rate suppression. At the same time, the ratepayers of the selling utilities gain because part of their electricity supply is subsidized by profits from purchases. Ironically, the big losers in the purchased power game are ratepayers of the buying utility, who end up paying more for electricity because their regulatory commissions have tried to hold down rates.

In summary, the rate-suppression/capital-minimization syndrome creates a fuel penalty that is equivalent to the savings forgone when a utility (1) fails to build new power plants to displace petroleum, (2) refuses to convert existing coal-capable oil-fired plants back to coal, (3) does not pursue conservation to the greatest economic extent possible; and (4) relies on purchased power that is more expensive than building its own capacity. In Chapter 7 we shall attempt a more exact assessment of the magnitude of this penalty levied on consumers, but we have already seen that it is likely to be on the order of tens of billions of dollars for America's ratepayers. The bad news for ratepayers does not end here, however, as our next two chapters demonstrate.

27. For example, Arizona Power and Light sells electricity for about 5.0¢ per kilowatt hour while producing it for approximately 3.3¢. The cost of self-generated electricity to a purchasing utility would average 3.1¢ per kilowatt hour for nuclear units, and 3.5¢ for coal units (industry averages from the Atomic Industrial Forum, year-end surveys.)

4 THE COST-OF-CAPITAL PENALTY

The second regulatory penalty created by the rate-suppression/capital-minimization syndrome is the cost-of-capital penalty. This penalty arises because investors associate rate suppression with the increased regulatory risk of earning below market returns; on Wall Street, this increased risk manifests itself in the form of higher interest charges for borrowed funds and lower stock prices. At the same time, to the extent that rate-suppressed utilities are forced to delay ongoing construction projects because of financial constraints, the real capital costs of completing the plants plus the total interest charges rise.

THE COST OF HIGH RISK

In the electric utility industry, roughly half of all new investment is financed through borrowed funds raised by selling bonds; the other half is financed primarily through equity funds, including both the issuance of new stock and the use of retained earnings (retained earnings represent the profits a company does not distribute to shareholders as dividends).[1]

Research and experience have shown that utilities operating in states whose PUCs suppress rates pay more for both the debt capital

1. *Electrical World* (March 1983): 81.

(borrowed funds) and equity capital (stock issues) they raise for new investment. There are logical reasons why this should be so. In general, people and institutions allow others to use their money only if they think that use will bring them a profit. Although most investments involve some degree of risk, that degree varies. As an incentive to attract capital, riskier ventures must offer the promise of greater profits. Therefore, when a company that is viewed as being a risky investment needs to borrow money, it must offer to pay a higher return on that money than would a company that is seen as a safer investment. That higher return, or so-called risk premium, takes the form of higher interest rates on borrowed funds and lower stock prices.

In the case of borrowed funds (or debt capital), utilities regularly sell their bonds through Wall Street investment houses. The interest rate that a utility must offer in order to sell its bonds to investors is determined by its bond rating. That rating, in turn, is set by Wall Street, with the firms of Moody's and Standard & Poor's being the two most influential bond raters. Bond ratings give investors a signal of a utility's ability to pay its debt. They are based on factors such as the utility's expected rate of return and its coverage ratio (the ratio of the company's earnings before interest and taxes to its interest charges for the period), factors that are heavily dependent on PUC regulatory treatment.

For example, the higher the return a utility is expected to earn, the more funds it will have on hand to service its debt and the less risky it will be to investors. Similarly, a higher coverage ratio means that the utility has a larger cushion of earnings to pay its debt; again, that means less risk. The relation of these factors to rate suppression is clear: When a utility operates in a rate-suppressive regulatory environment, its expected return and its coverage ratio tend to be lower and the utility is a riskier investment.

The ratings that Wall Street assigns utilities in an effort to quantify where they fall on the risk spectrum range from the lowest-risk, highest-quality, investment-grade AAA category to the higher-risk, substandard, or speculative categories of BBB and below. In 1970 Standard & Poors rated 120 out of 130 utilities as A or above, which placed them at investment grade or better.[2] However, after a decade of

---

2. Standard & Poor's bond guide. See also Leonard S. Hynan, *America's Electric Utilities: Past, Present, and Future.* (Arlington, Virg.: Public Utilities Reports, 1983).

Figure 4–1.   Changes in Utility Bond Ratings, 1980–82.

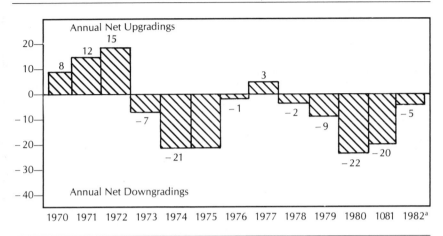

^aFirst half of 1982.
Source: *Standard & Poor's Bond Guide, 1962–1982.*

rate suppression, utility bond ratings have slumped. As Figure 4–1 shows, in every year but one since the Arab oil embargo, more utility bonds have been downgraded than have been upgraded. The mid-1970s and early 1980s, in particular, witnessed downgradings in unprecedented numbers. According to the consulting firm Booz, Allen & Hamilton, Standard & Poors made 100 more downgradings of utility bonds between 1973 and 1981 than upgradings.[3]

Not surprisingly, most of these bond deratings occurred for utilities operating in states with the most rate-suppressive PUCs.[4] As Figure 4-2 shows, in 1978, 90 percent of the utilities with Standard & Poor's ratings of A to BBB were in jurisdictions with an "unfavorable" regulatory climate, while only 13 percent of the utilities with higher-quality AAA or AA ratings were regulated by PUCs ranked "unfavorable."

Today, only 80 utility companies hold a rating of A or better, while the number below A has more than quadrupled (from 10 to 47) in the past ten years. The median in 1972 was AA; in 1983, it was A. As of September 30, 1983, of the 75 largest investor-owned utilities, only one company, Texas Utilities, held a AAA rating, while seven companies, Long Island Lighting Company, Public Service of Indiana,

3. *The Financial Health of the Electric Utility Industry*, prepared for the U.S. Department of Energy by Booz, Allen & Hamilton, Inc.
4. Ibid.

Figure 4–2. Utility Bond Ratings and Regulatory Climate.

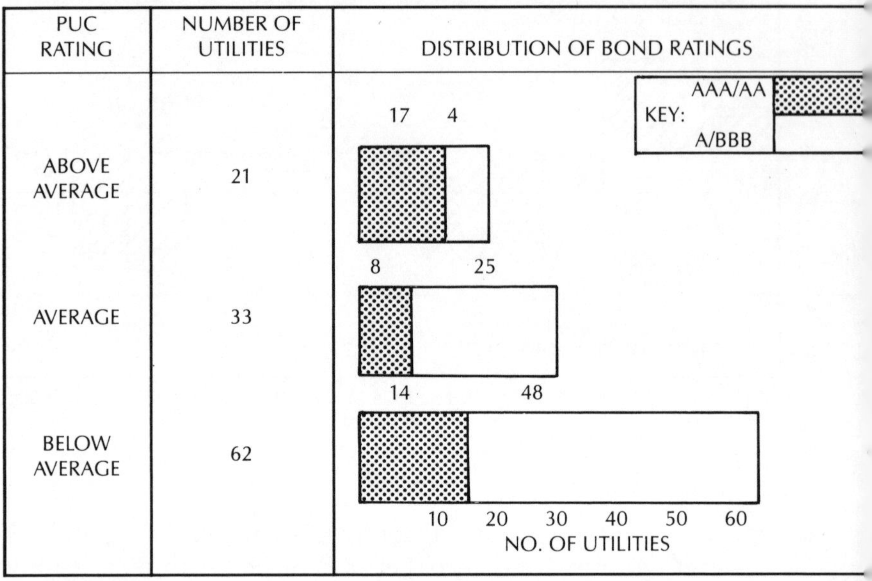

PUC RATING	NUMBER OF UTILITIES	DISTRIBUTION OF BOND RATINGS
ABOVE AVERAGE	21	17 4 KEY: AAA/AA / A/BBB 8 25
AVERAGE	33	14 48
BELOW AVERAGE	62	10 20 30 40 50 60 NO. OF UTILITIES

Source: Booz, Allen & Hamilton, Inc.

Public Service of New Hampshire, Cincinnati Gas & Electric, Dayton Power & Light, United Illuminating, and Consumers Power, held BB ratings.[5] (LILCO's infamous financial problems primarily center around its difficulties in getting its Shoreham nuclear plant into the rate base.) Although the trend has slowed somewhat, Wall Street investment companies continue to downgrade many utilities' bond ratings, and downgradings still outnumber upgradings.

The contribution of a bond derating to the cost-of-capital penalty seems most significant when translated into dollars and cents. To illustrate, let's assume that a utility's bond rating fell from AAA to BBB and that the company must issue $500 million in bonds for a new coal plant. Let's assume also that the interest rate on a BBB bond is two hundred basis points higher than on a AAA bond—say, 14 percent as opposed to 12 percent. This two-percentage-point gap, which approximates the average spread witnessed over the past five years, means that the BBB-rated utility has to pay $10 million more per year in interest charges than if it were rated AAA. These charges will be

5. Standard & Poor's bond guide.

passed on to consumers in the form of rate increases worth $300 million over the thirty-year life of the bonds. As testimony to this cost-of-capital penalty, a report by the Texas PUC demonstrates that utilities with higher bond ratings provide lower-cost electricity to their ratepayers.[6]

But higher interest charges aren't the only fallout from rate suppression; the *availability* of debt capital is also affected. Rate-suppressed utilities typically have less debt capital available to them because one of the largest groups of investors in utility bonds is institutions, particularly pension funds; as mentioned earlier, the Employment Retirement Income and Securities Act prohibits such investors from purchasing low-rated bonds.

The same problem of higher capital costs arises, albeit in a more indirect way, when a utility issues stock to raise investment funds. As previously discussed, the price of a stock depends primarily on the return investors expect to earn; this return comes in the form of both dividends and capital gains and is based on the ratio of the income realized by the stock to the stock's price. Rate suppression affects this relationship between expected returns and stock prices in several ways.

First, to the extent that rate suppression results in an actual return that is lower than the expected return, the price of the stock falls. The reason is that new investors will always expect a certain return, and if the income the utility earns does not generate such a return, then what that return is being earned on (the stock price) must fall. For example, suppose investors expect a 10 percent return on a utility stock that sells for $100. Assuming that the stock has no appreciation and that all earnings are distributed as dividends, the utility must deliver $10 in dividends to realize this return. But if it delivers only $9, the stock price will fall to $90, so that new investors would continue to realize a 10 percent return.

Second, as rate suppression increases, so too does the perceived risk of investing in the utility's stock. This risk comes in the form of a possible *further* drop in stock prices and the concomitant potential capital loss to existing shareholders. But this increased perception of risk raises the return expected by investors; according to a number of studies, the resultant risk premium adds another 100 to 200 basis

6. Samuel Hadaway, Brenton Heidbrecht, and Jeffrey Nash, "A Cost-Benefit Analysis of Alternative Bond Ratings Among Electric Utility Companies in Texas" (Public Utilities Commission of Texas, Economic Research Division, December 1982), p. 13.

points to the expected return.[7] (A 100-basis-point increase represents a one percentage point increase in the interest rate, e.g., from 13 percent to 14 percent.) This higher expected return puts further downward pressure on the stock.

For a rate-suppressed utility in search of equity financing, the result, then, is a double whammy of lower stock prices and what amounts to the same thing, higher expected returns to attract investors. For the utility, this means it must sell more shares to raise the same amount of funds. For existing shareholders, it means that raising funds by selling new shares of stock is almost certain to devalue or dilute the value of their shares by driving down the stock price—and hence, any potential capital gains.

Accordingly, as with debt financing, rate suppression not only raises the cost of equity capital but also reduces its availability. Disgruntled shareholders who fear a devaluation of their holdings put pressure on—and sometimes sue—management to prevent it from selling any new stock. A case in point is one large shareholder who successfully blocked the issuance of 1.5 million common shares of Idaho Power. And a large shareholder of Pacific Gas & Electric has sued that company and the California PUC for allowing the sale of that utility's stock at prices below book value.[8] In the future, as devaluation continues to occur, we can expect to see more such actions.

THE COST OF DELAYED AND CANCELED PLANTS

Besides the effects of rate suppression on a utility's cost of debt and equity capital, a more subtle penalty arises. As part of their response to rate suppression, utility company executives often delay or cancel construction plans. Reports of slowed construction and cancellations continually pop up in the business sections of newspapers. As mentioned in Chapter 2, in 1980 utilities canceled or delayed over half the

7. Jeffrey A. Dubin and Peter Navarro, "Regulatory Climate and the Cost of Capital" (Harvard University discussion paper E–82–03, April 1982); and Robert R. Trout, "The Regulatory Factor and Electric Utility Common Stock Investment Values," *Public Utilities Fortnightly* (November 22, 1979): 28.

8. "Big PG&E Shareholder Sues Utility, PUC for Below-Book Sales of Stock," *Electrical Week* (June 21, 1982): 1.

new power plants they had planned to come on line by 1989.[9] In 1981 and 1982, U.S. utilities canceled 47 major power plants that would have boosted capacity 50 million kilowatts (8 percent of U.S. capacity) at an estimated cost of $10 billion.[10] From 1974 through 1981, 39 coal plants were canceled and 335 were delayed; the average delay has increased steadily since 1976, from a mean of 13.6 months to over 21 months.[11]

When utility executives delay or cancel their construction plans as part of a capital minimization strategy, they often incur a cost-of-capital penalty. It has several components. Most obviously, when a utility company invests money to construct a plant and then decides to cancel it, the company forfeits the funds already invested. From 1972 through 1982, 100 nuclear plants were canceled, for a total of 109,754 megawatts.[12] In 1982 alone, there were 18 cancellations amounting to 21,937 megawatts; construction had started on half of them.[13]

The total cost of abandoning these plants is estimated to be in the billions. Private, investor-owned utilities incurred a loss of nearly $6 billion from their share of cancellations through 1982.[14] Virginia Electric Power's cancellation of North Anna 3 in 1983 incurred some $500 million in abandonment costs; that same year, Northern Indiana Public Service canceled its Bailly plant at a cost of $200 million.[15] Table 4-1 lists other abandonment costs, including that of Boston Edison's aforementioned Pilgrim 2, whose cancellation cost equals roughly $400 million.

As if those figures weren't high enough, the Energy Information Administration of the Department of Energy estimates the total cost of future nuclear plant cancellations to be between $4.5 and $8.1 billion. That burden would not be distributed evenly. Ratepayers in the Southeast alone could bear $1.5 to $4.6 billion in abandonment

9. *The Nation's Electric Future: Perspectives on the Issue of Electricity Supply Sufficiency* (Washington, D.C.: U.S. Department of Energy, Office of Policy, Planning and Analysis, February 1982), p. 15.

10. "The Vicious Circle That Utilities Can't Seem to Break," *Business Week* (May 23, 1983): 178.

11. U.S. Department of Energy, Energy Information Administration, "Delays and Cancellations of Coal-Fired Generating Capacity" (Washington, D.C., July 1983).

12. U.S. Department of Energy, Energy Information Administration, "Nuclear Plant Cancellations: Causes, Costs, and Consequences" (Washington, D.C., April 198).

13. Ibid.

14. Ibid.

15. Ibid. Figures are in 1982 dollars.

Table 4–1.   Status and Abandonment Costs of Some Canceled Nuclear Units.

Plant Name	Date of Cancellation	Percentage Complete	Abandonment Costs[a] (in millions of 1982 dollars)
Pilgrim 2	9/81	0	$410
Sterling	2/80	0	151
Atlantic 1 and 2	1/78	0	461
Hope Creek 2	12/81	19	432
Forked River 1	11/80	6	489
North Anna 3	11/82	8	504
Allens Creek 1	8/82	0	360

[a]These costs were obtained from a variety of sources: FERC Form 1 submissions, annual reports, regulatory commission opinions, and utility executives.

Source: *Nuclear Plant Cancellations, Causes and Costs* (Washington, D.C.: U.S. Department of Energy, Energy Information Administration, April 1983).

costs; New England ratepayers could suffer $749 million in abandonment costs.

Who pays for the cancellations? In some cases, shareholders bear the burden in the form of reduced earnings and lower stock prices. But in many cases, consumers have been forced to share part of the loss. For example, after Boston Edison canceled Pilgrim 2, the Massachusetts PUC subsequently ruled that Edison would be allowed to recoup $305 million, including taxes, over a thirteen-year period. This ruling raised consumer rates an average of 4.6 percent exclusive of fuel costs.[16]

Construction *delays* can be equally costly. When a utility is forced to delay construction of a plant already underway, it must pay interest on the funds it has invested for a longer period of time (i.e., the length of the delay). The interest charges and other costs that a utility must pay during plant construction are called the carrying charges. When construction plans drag, the increase in carrying charges can add a sizable chunk to the overall cost of the plant—and to the rates consumers will pay for use of that plant.

Delays can also raise the total cost of a plant if the real cost of construction materials rises over time. Over the past decade, the

16. DPU Order 906, dated April 30, 1982.

increased cost of "bricks and mortar" has indeed outpaced inflation, so every day of delay adds additional real costs to the plant's final price tag.

A classic example of the effect that delay can have on total construction costs is provided by a comparison of two nuclear units, the Millstone 2 unit of Northeast Utilities and the Shoreham plant of Long Island Lighting Company (LILCO). Both units were started at the same time, both were the same size, and their original cost estimates were very similar. Millstone 2 was completed in 1975 at a cost of $434 million. Shoreham, however, has been plagued by numerous delays and financial difficulties within LILCO, and its estimated cost is now over $4 billion.[17] In a similar vein, the Philadelphia Electric Company recently announced an 18-month delay in construction of its 1,050 megawatt Limerick 2 nuclear unit and estimated that this delay would increase the cost of the plant by $550 million.[18]

Still further evidence is provided by the Energy Information Administration, which has found that delays and cancellations of coal-fired units do indeed result in higher per-unit costs: Those units that came on line with no delays during the 1977–79 period experienced a 6.8 percent annual cost increase, while those experiencing a delay of three years or more had a 17.9 percent per year increase.[19]

In summary, rate suppression imposes a cost-of-capital penalty through three channels: It boosts the cost of both debt and equity by raising perceived investor risk; it leads to cancellations that result in abandonment costs; and it leads to delays that boost both the carrying charges and the real price tag on a new plant. In all cases, it is electricity consumers who eventually assume a large part of the cost-of-capital burden.

17. Long Island Lighting Company community affairs office.
18. Press release, Philadelphia Electric Company, Public Information Division, January 24, 1984.
19. U.S. Department of Energy, "Delays and Cancellations of Coal-Fired Generating Capacity."

5 THE RELIABILITY PENALTY

The third regulatory penalty created by the rate-suppression/capital-minimization syndrome is the reliability penalty. It arises when utilities fail to build enough new capacity to meet load growth and when utility executives, trying to protect their companies' earnings, cut back too far on operating and maintenance expenses.

THE RISK OF UNDERBUILDING

Prior to the 1970s, utility executives and engineers lived in a predictable world where the demand for electricity increased at roughly 7 percent a year with little fluctuation. Utility planners could plot this steady growth by drawing a straight, upward sloping line on a graph. Meeting customer needs was a simple matter of planning new power plants to meet the next point on the demand graph.

Today, the predictability of new capacity needs has gone the way of twenty five-cent-per-gallon gasoline, as soaring energy costs and repeated doses of recession and "stagflation" have drastically altered the formerly linear pattern of electricity demand growth.[1] As a result of conservation and the pressures of recession, the pre-1970s average

1. *Stagflation* refers to the simultaneous existence of recession and rapid inflation, a condition thought improbable by economists before the 1970s.

Table 5-1.   Annual Growth in Electricity Demand, 1960–1983.

Year	Percentage Growth Rate	Year	Percentage Growth Rate
1960–61	4.6	1970–71	5.3
1961–62	7.6	1971–72	8.4
1962–63	7.2	1972–73	6.7
1963–64	7.1	1973–74	0.2
1964–65	7.4	1974–75	2.6
1965–66	8.8	1975–76	6.3
1966–67	6.0	1976–77	4.6
1967–68	8.7	1977–78	4.1
1968–69	9.0	1978–79	2.2
1969–70	6.3	1979–80	0.8
		1980–81	– 2.2
		1981–82	3.6
		1982–83	3.7

Source: Edison Electric Institute, *Statistical Yearbook of the Electric Utility Industry/1982* (Washington, D.C.: EEI, October 1983), no. 50; and North American Electric Reliability Council, *Electric Power Supply and Demand 1984–1983* (July 1983).

rate of growth in electricity demand has been cut almost in half to the rate of 3.6 percent. Moreover, this average rate is the product of very erratic growth rates in individual years, as Table 5-1 illustrates. In some years, such as 1972, 1973, and 1976, electricity demand growth has been as high as 6.3 to 8.4 percent. But in recession-plagued years such as 1974 and 1980, it has been close to zero and in 1981–82 even negative.

In thinking about the reliability penalty, one important question to consider is to what extent conservation will continue to hold down the growth rate in electricity demand. In some quarters it is argued that through conservation and a leveling off of population, zero electricity demand growth is both feasible and desirable. In such a world, new power plants would be needed only to replace whatever capacity wears out.

But most analysts are not so sanguine about conservation's potential to bring electricity demand growth to a complete halt. These analysts see the low growth rates in electricity demand during the 1970s and early 1980s as being attributable as much to economic recession as to conservation, and they point to the rebound of demand growth in periods of economic expansion to buttress their argument. These rebounds are marked by the higher growth rates in Table 5-1, such as the 6.3 and 4.6 rates in 1975-76 and 1976-77 and the latest case in point, the improved 3.6 percent annual growth rate observed in the later stages of Reagan's "economic recovery." (In the second half of 1983, in fact, electricity demand grew at a rate of about 8.5 percent over that experienced in the second half of 1982.)

Moreover, many analysts believe that the "quantum leap" gains from conservation have already been made so that its ability to drive demand growth down further is weakening. That is, conservation has occurred and will continue to occur because of increased energy prices, improved technology, and increased availability of information (e.g., appliance labels). Also, subsidies in the form of tax credits and the like will continue to encourage conservation. But the abrupt change in electricity demand that the initial introduction of these energy-efficiency options brought about is not likely to be repeated. Therefore, although efforts to conserve electricity use will continue, the rate of growth of conservation is unlikely to duplicate that of the early 1970s. It follows that the impact of conservation on electricity demand is likely to hold steady rather than push the growth rate in demand down further.

Accordingly, most analysts predict that demand for electricity will continue to grow at a rate of at least 3 percent per year and, if the economy continues to recover over the next few years, perhaps even higher. Among those making such predictions are the Department of Energy and the Electric Power Research Institute. Data Resources, Inc. makes a slightly more conservative estimate; it forecasts a 2.67 percent growth in demand through the year 2000.

Within the context of the rate-suppression/capital-minimization syndrome, these predictions are foreboding. For even with the demand growth of an earlier era cut by more than half, the required investment in new power plant construction to meet our future electricity needs is staggering.

At present, the value of utility assets exceeds $280 billion. But just to meet the requirements of a 3 percent annual growth rate, by the year 2000 the utility industry will have to build over 400 gigawatts of capacity, which is a hefty addition to its current capacity of roughly

650 gigawatts.[2] To accomplish this expansion, it will have to invest a cumulative total of approximately $1 trillion (in constant 1982 dollars). That figure dwarfs the industry's existing asset base, which was $300 billion in 1981. Moreover, to meet future demand, the utility industry will have to begin to undertake such investments now. It takes a minimum of six to eight years to build a new power plant, and these lead times can, for a variety of financial and regulatory reasons, stretch to between ten and fourteen years.

Is there any evidence to suggest that the utility industry is moving forward to meet forecast demand? There is considerable evidence on the industry's prospects for supplying electricity, but it points to the unfortunate conclusion that some regions of the United States will be woefully short of new capacity to keep the lights on if the utility industry continues its unprecedented trend toward the cancellation, delay, and deferral of new construction. To reiterate some facts mentioned in Chapter 3, over half of the new coal and nuclear plant capacity scheduled through 1988 has been delayed an average of 20 months, and from 1977 to 1982, about 140 generating units representing some 150,000 megawatts of electricity were canceled or deferred indefinitely. Further, no new nuclear units have been ordered since 1978, no new order for a major generating project was placed in 1982, and only one order was placed in 1983.

According to the Department of Energy, this pattern of cancellations, delays, and deferrals will almost certainly lead to serious supply shortages in some states and regions of the country by the early 1990s.[3] For example, if electricity demand grows at only 2 percent a year, utilities in Kansas, Arkansas, Louisiana, the Dakotas, Minnesota, Iowa, Nebraska, and parts of Missouri and Mississippi will face a serious shrinkage of the reserve capacity (or "reserve margin") they have as insurance against power failures, a shrinkage which could lead to serious shortages, blackouts, and brownouts. Two of our largest states—Texas and California—will definitely face severe shortages in the 1990s if the trend of capital minimization continues.[4]

2. *The Future of Electric Power in America: Economic Supply for Economic Growth* (Washington, D.C.: U.S. Department of Energy, Office of Policy, Planning and Analysis, June 1983), p. ES–18. Estimate includes capacity needed to replace retired, uneconomical, and inefficient capacity and allows for a 20 percent reserve margin.

3. *Future of Electric Power*, ES–9. They are already short of *economic* power (Texas relies heavily on natural gas, while California is heavily dependent on oil and gas.). Texas electricity supply is noneconomic in the sense that rates would be cheaper over time if the utilities replaced much of their petroleum capacity with nonpetroleum plants, e.g., coal plants.

4. Ibid.

RELIABILITY VERSUS ECONOMIC RESERVE MARGINS

The seriousness of this situation in some regions of the country is masked by the fact that when the capacity situation is assessed from a national perspective, there seems to be a surplus of power plants. To avoid succumbing to the illusion of excess capacity and to fully understand the reliability penalty, it is useful to know how reliability is measured.

The most frequently used measure is a utility's *reserve margin*, which measures the amount of extra capacity that a utility has standing idle but that can be called into service should some plant or plants in the system fail. It is the percentage of capacity a utility has over and above its peak, or maximum, demand.[5]

The traditional guideline is that a 20 percent reserve margin is sufficient to maintain system reliability. Margins above that rule-of-thumb level are supposed to signal "goldplating"—a utility's efforts to cram excess capacity into its rate base in order to boost its profits. But reserve margin calculations can be and have been interpreted erroneously.

For example, projections of the national average reserve margin for 1990 are above 20 percent (assuming that the demand growth rate is 3 percent or less). These figures provide no hint of a problem. But they are deceptive, because the "national average" is a combination of both the seemingly high reserve margins in some of the more petroleum dependent regions as well as the margins for those regions where an underlying reliability problem exists. When the high margins of such areas as New England and the Tennessee Valley are averaged in with lower margins elsewhere, the national average comes out at an apparently comfortable 33 percent.

This figure ignores the reality that the "national" electricity grid that transmits power is not national at all. Rather, it is a loosely and incompletely connected *regional* grid system that lacks the lines and interconnections for adequately linking the supply-rich regions with the supply-poor ones.

For example, the transmission lines connecting the northwestern United States to California, which is a major potential victim of

5. The accuracy of this reserve margin measure of realiability is a matter of some controversy. See, for example, *The National Electric Reliability Study: Final Report.* (Washington, D.C.: U.S. Department of Energy, Assistant Secretary for Environment, Safety and Emergency Preparedness, April 1981).

capacity shortfalls, have limited capacity, although they are likely to be expanded from 1,600 megawatts to 3,100 megawatts. Worse off is Texas, which for longstanding political reasons has a completely independent grid that renders it almost totally incapable of receiving power from other states.

Nor is the solution simply to build enough transmission lines to connect the have and have-not regions. Most of the extra capacity in the United States will, by the 1990s, be expensive oil- and gas-fired power plants. This is a subtle but extremely important point: while such power might be useful in a crisis (and probably will be used in a crisis, further raising the fuel penalty imposed on consumers), building transmission lines—which themselves require considerable investment— would be far more expensive than building new nonpetroleum capacity in the regions where shortages are anticipated.

The combustion-turbine strategy is not an economic alternative to electricity in short supply either. Under such a strategy, utilities would build oil- and gas-fired turbines to fill the breach. Since these turbines are far less capital-intensive than, say, a coal plant, they can be up and running within a year or two. The obvious drawback of "CTs" is that because they are petroleum-dependent, they produce electricity at a cost two to three times that of a coal plant. Would the industry install such petroleum guzzlers to keep the lights on? Most likely, since such a strategy was adopted in a similar period of crisis in the late 1960s and early 1970s when the industry purchased and installed some 35 gigawatts (the equivalent of 30 large coal plants) to ensure reliable service.[6] While these combustion turbines saved on the reliability penalty, the burden of the shortage was merely shifted to the fuel penalty—and consumer bills. It would be unfortunate to repeat this mistake.

The reserve-margin rule is frequently invoked by opponents of new power plant construction who argue that conservation has made such construction unnecessary. But this concept, if adhered to, will have severe consequences for both ratepayers and the nation.

At one hearing before the Connecticut Public Utility Commission, the state's public counsel and PUC staff strongly opposed Northeast Utilities' request for a rate hike that would have facilitated the completion of Millstone 3, a large nuclear plant. The PUC's argu-

6. Testimony of J. Steven Herod on behalf of the United States Department of Energy before the State of Connecticut Department of Business Regulation, Division of Public Utility Control, 1979.

Figure 5–1. Economic versus Reliability-Reserve Margins
New England.

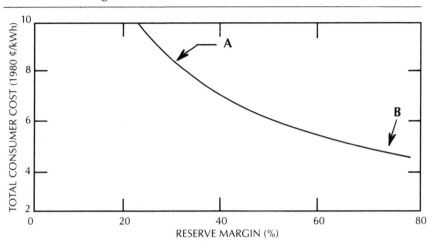

Source: The National Electric Reliability Study, Vol.1, February 1980

ment against the increase was that the addition of Millstone would have boosted Northeast's reserve margin to over 40 percent, excessive in its view. But according to testimony delivered by the U.S. Department of Energy in that hearing, the actual excess capacity would be noneconomic oil capacity, and the resultant savings of having the nuclear unit displace the oil capacity would actually reduce electricity rates below what they otherwise would be.[7]

The crucial point this example illustrates is that the postembargo economics of petroleum displacement require a more modern view of reserve margins. It is no longer correct to think of the 20 percent rule as etched in stone. Instead, it should be regarded as merely a lower bound, below which no utility would want to fall for reliability reasons but above which utilities may want to go for economic reasons. Thus, a utility heavily dependent on petroleum can in some cases build a new nonpetroleum power plant and double its reserve margin but still save ratepayers money; the petroleum plants would be put on standby, used sparingly (if at all), and gradually retired.

The Department of Energy's *National Electric Reliability Study* has brought this important distinction between "reliability" and "economic" reserve margins into sharp focus.[8] The study analyzed a

7. *National Electric Reliability Study.*

8. Ibid, p. 83. It should be emphasized that these lower rates *include* the construction costs of the new plants.

number of regions in the country to determine their economic reserve margins—that is, those margins that provided the lowest cost electricity generation. It found *no* relationship between the 20 percent reliability rule of thumb and the economic reserve margin. Instead, DOE found that economic reserve margins appear to be highly variable and largely dependent on the amount of petroleum in a utility's or a region's generation mix. The new rule of thumb is that the economic reserve margin rises with the amount of petroleum in the generation mix.

Figure 5-1 illustrates the principle of economic reserve margins for New England, a region that depends on oil for more than 60 percent of its electricity generation. The vertical axis measures the cost to consumers per kilowatt hour, and the horizontal axis measures reserve margins. As new coal and nuclear capacity is added to displace existing oil plants, the region exceeds the 20 percent reliability reserve mark, yet electricity costs steadily decline. At a 27 percent reserve margin, the cost of electricity is 9.9 cents per kilowatt hour (see point A on the graph). This is the margin New England is scheduled to maintain through the next decade. If New England were to instead pursue the economics of petroleum displacement and build to a 78 percent reserve margin (point B), it could cut the cost of electricity by more than half, to 4.6 cents per kilowatt hour.[9] Similarly, DOE found that for petroleum-dependent utilities in the southern California/southern Nevada region, the economic reserve margin was 70 percent, while in the Florida-Southern Company region, the lowest electricity costs were achieved at a reserve margin of 49 percent.

Thus, load growth is not the only reason to build new power plants. And reserve capacity above the percentage traditionally prescribed for reliability reasons is not necessarily extravagant. On the contrary, even very high reserve margins can be uneconomic. This fact lends justification for adding new capacity to displace petroleum.

Unfortunately, many regulators are reluctant to accept an economic determination of desirable reserve margins. State commissions typically allow in a utility's rate base only those assets that are "used and useful." If a utility builds a new nonpetroleum plant to substitute for an existing, economically obsolete petroleum plant, it faces a major risk: If the commission adheres to the traditional

9. Ibid, p. 83. It should be emphasized that these lower rates *include* the construction costs of the new plants.

reliability view of reserve margins, it may deem the plant unnecessary from a reliability standpoint and not allow it into the rate base. Indeed, a 1980 decision by the Missouri Public Service Commission not to allow an *operating* coal plant into Kansas City Power & Light's rate base is evidence of the seriousness of this risk. The specter of being denied a return on new, petroleum-displacing capacity provides utility managers with yet another disincentive to undertake capacity expansion to eliminate petroleum economically.

Partially as a result of utilities' attempts to adopt this new concept of economic reserve margins, some petroleum-dependent regions of the country now have reserve margins well in excess of 20 percent. For example, in New York the reserve margin is about 40 percent, while in the Dakotas, Minnesota, Iowa, and Nebraska it is 44 percent.[10] On the other hand, current reserve margins in California are not only below what is economic but also below the old 20 percent reliability rule.[11]

THE O&M SQUEEZE

The failure of the utility industry to build new power plants in the face of forecast growth in electricity demand is not the only threat to a reliable supply of electricity. A more subtle source of the reliability penalty is rate suppression's squeeze on the operations and maintenance expenses of utilities. This O&M squeeze affects not only those regions where available capacity is projected to be low but all regions, most ominously those where significant nuclear capacity exists.

When utilities are restricted from earning a rate of return that keeps pace with changes in economic conditions, ratepayers get a good deal—at first. But as utilities begin to feel the stranglehold of rate suppression, they look for ways to cut back on their expenses so that they can keep paying shareholder dividends and interest on borrowed funds. At first these cutbacks are salutary. Some of the fat—notorious in regulated industries—is trimmed. But once the first trims have been made, persistent rate suppression inevitably leads to cutting into muscle and bone. Work crews are reduced in size, rou-

10. *Future of Electric Power*, p. 4-39.
11. Ibid.

tine checks of plant equipment are made less often, power plant parts are used longer, and with these cutbacks comes an inevitable increase in power supply interruptions.

Examples of utility companies that have trimmed their operating and maintenance expenditures are numerous. In May 1983 Pacific Power & Light Company announced its intention to reduce its 5,000-pers on work force by some 400 people. It eliminated jobs as they became open and offered early retirement incentives in an effort to cut its operating budget by $49 million. The O&M budget was cut by $15 million, and almost 200 of the jobs eliminated were groundmen, linemen, and service personnel.[12] Similarly, in a direct regulatory O&M squeeze, the Massachusetts Department of Public Utilities recently reviewed Boston Edison's request for a $74 million rate hike. It granted the increase, but only after cutting that request by 58 percent. The largest cut—$15 million—was in Edison's allocation for operating and maintenance costs.[13] This O&M squeeze is exacerbated by the rapid rise in utility O&M expenses. For fossil fuel plants, these expenses more than tripled over the past decade.[14]

Perhaps not surprisingly, both the number and average duration of utility power failures have risen over the last decade along with rate suppression and the O&M squeeze. For example, of eight utilities surveyed by the Utility Systems and Emergency Communications Division of the Department of Energy, the total number of interruptions of one minute or more increased from 52,000 in 1974 to 81,000 in 1978.[15] The average duration of those interruptions was 130 customer minutes in 1974 and 170 customer minutes in 1978.[16] Of all interruptions of power reported between 1970 and 1979 to the Utility Systems and Emergency Communications Division in the Office of Emergency Operations, Assistant Secretary for Environment, and Safety and Emergency Preparedness, 75 percent were due to problems related to facilities maintenance or operation and coordination. Only 25 percent were initiated by causes external to the utility. For

12. Pacific Power & Light Company information office.
13. Boston Edison's Public Information Office.
14. Scott A. Fenn, *America's Electric Utilities* (Washington, D.C.: Investor Responsibility Research Center, 1983), p. 26.
15. S.P. Walldorf and L.C. Markel, "The Electric Utility Industry—Past and Present: Background Information for the National Electric Reliability Study" (Technical Study Reports, October 1980).
16. *National Electric Reliability Study*, p. 44.

many of those interruptions, preventive maintenance work would have made the disturbances less severe and in some cases would have kept the whole system from going down.[17]

This evidence is corroborated by a study performed by economist Marie Corio, who examined the relationship of reduced O&M expenditures and the probability of power failures. According to Corio: "If a utility's earnings are squeezed, poor (power plant) unit performance follows—although it takes a couple of years for this to become apparent in lower (equipment) availability and...higher costs to the ratepayer."[18]

In an industry that relies on nuclear power for over 13 percent of its generation, this O&M squeeze is of particular concern. But when it comes to the reliability penalty, the potential damage goes beyond the meltdown scare; according to the Electric Power Research Institute, the reliability risks and costs of underbuilding electricity capacity may be far more severe than those of overbuilding electricity capacity.[19]

ASSESSING THE RELIABILITY PENALTY

The effects of the reliability penalty are unquestionably the most difficult to measure. Except for isolated and infrequent episodes of blackouts or brownouts, Americans have enjoyed extremely reliable power throughout this century; consequently, there is little experience on which to base estimates of the costs of electricity shortages. Still, the few incidents that have occurred give us clues as to who will be affected, how the effects will be manifested, and how high the costs of the dimming of America might be. For example, in July of 1977, New York City suffered a blackout that lasted twenty five hours when lightning cut the power at Consolidated Edison's Indian Point nuclear plant. Many retail businesses had to close, as did Wall Street, because its high-speed electronic communications network was inoperable. To protect the closed businesses and darkened

17. *National Electric Reliability Study*, p. 43.
18. Marie R. Corio, "Why Is the Performance of Electric Generating Units Declining?" *Public Utilities Fortnightly* (April 29, 1982): 25.
19. *Generating Capacity in U.S. Electric Utilities* (Palo Alto, Calif.: Electrical Power Research Institute, EA–2639–SR, October 1982).

streets, local police and firemen worked overtime, and the state police were called in. A study of the effects of that outage found that New York City had to pay its police and firemen some $12 million in extra wages, and Westchester County paid about $100,000.[20] These two figures exclude the cost of arresting, processing, and jailing some 3,776 persons arrested during the looting and general chaos. And of course the value of the two lives that were lost and hundreds of injuries sustained cannot be measured in dollars.

Further, the Emergency Aid Commission granted $2.9 million in cash assistance to help businesses get reestablished. The U.S. Department of Labor made available $11.2 million in grants and loans, and the Small Business Administration received claims for damage totaling $75.8 million. Some $30 million in claims were filed with private insurers.

These losses are indicative of how wide the ramifications of such an event can actually be. Other indirect losses might include overtime payments to production workers, and hospital employees, and restoration of the failed electrical capacity. Consumers would of course pay their share of these costs as well as the cost of food that spoils in their unpowered refrigerators and freezers. They would also suffer the stress associated with the increased dnager of vandalism and the inconvenience and discomfort of doing without electrically powered heating and cooling. For older people, the loss of heating and cooling can be especially dangerous in the hottest days of summer or the coldest days of winter, when power interruptions are most likely to occur.

In the summer of 1983, a twelve-block area of New York City's garment district lost power when a fire broke out in a Con Ed substation. The blackout lasted four days of a buying week, when thousands of merchants come to New York to buy apparel for their stores. A spokesperson for the Federation of Apparel Manufacturers said the outage cost the industry some $100 million in lost sales. Moreover, the city had to pay $854,000 in overtime wages to police the area, and the utility, of course, had to pay to repair the damaged equipment.

---

20. "The Cost of an Urban Blackout: The Consolidated Edison Blackout, July 13–14, 1977," study prepared by the Congressional Research Service, Library of Congress, for the U.S. House of Representatives Subcommittee on Energy and Power (Washington, D.C.: U.S. Government Printing Office, 1978).

Clearly, then, the reliability penalty will be borne by all sectors of the economy—residental, commercial, industrial, and even the government. Our experience with episodes of electricity-supply interruption, albeit limited, suggests that the price tag will be high. This is no less true in our increasingly high-tech, computerized, and, not coincidentally, electrified world where word processors, computers, and the telecommunications network are quite literally America's central nervous system.

BETWEEN COMPLACENCY AND CRYING WOLF

In considering the reliability penalty, one final comment is perhaps in order. America has never faced a serious electricity shortage. This is true despite occasional dire warnings by the electric utility industry that such shortages are just over the horizon. Unfortunately, the absence of serious shortages makes most of us oblivious to the dangers, just as most of us were unaware of the possibility of an oil embargo before 1973. Our resultant complacency is compounded by the industry's propensity to "cry wolf." But to paraphrase James Akins's comment on the Arab oil embargo, the rate-suppression/capital-minimization syndrome suggests that soon the wolf may really be here.[21] At least in some regions of the country, current forecasts point to exactly that conclusion.

The seriousness of such a conclusion behooves us to carefully assess the probability that the lights of America will actually flicker and dim. Given the recent proliferation of "quick and dirty" fixes such as expensive petroleum-fired combustion turbines and reserve petroleum capacity, we must also ask whether the lights going out is the real worry. Perhaps the dimming of America will occur in a more figurative sense, through an economically dark and drab future of soaring electricity rates, falling real incomes, fewer job opportunities, and slower growth.

Without an infallible crystal ball, the only way to predict what the future holds for us is to ask ourselves what must happen for electricity shortages first to occur and then to persist.

21. James E. Akins, "The Oil Crisis: This Time the Wolf Is Here," *Foreign Affairs* (April 1973): 462.

The first requirement is a continued growth in electricity demand in those regions most susceptible to supply shortages. Since the greatest levels of both economic and electricity demand growth are forecast for precisely those states and regions where average reliability reserve margins are lowest, it is reasonable to conclude that this requirement will be met.[22]

The second requirement is that utility executives in the most vulnerable regions must continue to pursue a strategy of capital minimization. That is, they must build no new plants (or fewer plants than necessary) to meet forecast demand. While again a crystal ball would be useful, the limited evidence we do have suggests that this requirement may be met as well, for in those vulnerable regions as in the rest of the country, new plants are also being cancelled, delayed, and deferred.

The third requirement is that utility executives must fail to react in time to prevent impending electricity shortages. From an economic viewpoint, that means in many cases failure to build new nonpetroleum plants such as coal capacity now and throughout the 1980s and 1990s. These plants would take anywhere from five to twelve years to complete and would be ready to meet growing demand in several decades to come.

From the standpoint of pure reliability, however, this reaction can also mean failure to build noneconomic combustion turbines even a few years before the actual shortages hit. Although electricity from these "CTs" would cost considerably more than new nonpetroleum plants (on the order of double to triple), they could in fact prevent the literal dimming of America.

It is likely that CTs will be built—but probably not until shortages actually hit. For one thing, federal law prohibits the construction of new petroleum capacity except in an emergency.[23] Prospective or anticipated shortages alone are not enough to allow a waiver. Moreover, building CTs, despite their low capital requirements, is inconsistent with a strategy of capital minimization, so utility executives are likely to postpone making the investment until the last minute. They might

---

22. For example, in California, where economic growth and electricity demand growth have been outpacing most of the country for many years, the reserve margin has been calculated to be 18.6. And in Texas, another high-growth area, the reserve margin has dropped to 24.0. (Preliminary survey data, 1983 reserve margins, Edison Electric Institute).

23. The Fuel Use Act of 1977.

even wait until their PUCs order them to build the CTs, because otherwise they run the risk that the PUCs won't allow the considerable fuel costs to be passed through to consumers.

Finally, utility executives have said on more than one occasion (although never publicly) that they are tired of environmentalists, anti-nuclear protestors, and consumer advocates telling them not to build new plants. Utility executives resent the implied usurpation of their prerogatives as managers and industry experts. In the same breath, they say that only a crisis such as a major electricity shortage will wake America up to the severe regulatory problems that exist. This "siege mentality" is, of course, a product of the pressures that the industry has been under for the last decade. It is as unconstructive as are the often bold accusations of the industry's critics. The bottom line of this seeming tug-of-war is a set of utility executives increasingly unwilling to make decisions that protect the public from a dark future but that are likely to draw the public's wrath.

Thus, shortages will occur in some regions, and these shortages will endure for one to two years—a short time in the scheme of things perhaps, but a fairly long time from the standpoint of politics. The literal dimming of America is therefore likely to be a relatively brief affair. Nonetheless, we should beware of the combustion turbine solution to the reliability problem, for as we shall see in the next several chapters, it will only hasten the economic dimming of America. It is to this more figurative though equally threatening result that we now turn.

III | THE HIGH COST OF LOW RATES

| Consumers: higher rates for less reliable service | National Energy Policy: increased dependence on foreign energy, reduced national security | National Economic Policy: lower growth, fewer jobs, higher inflation rate |

6 RATE SUPPRESSION AND NATIONAL POLICY GOALS

The rate-suppression/capital-minimization syndrome—working via the three regulatory penalties—poses a serious threat to our ability to meet a number of our national policy goals. In the realm of energy policy and national security, this syndrome interferes with the goals of reducing U.S. dependence on foreign oil and moderating political and military tensions in the Middle East. In the arena of economic policy, this syndrome threatens the goals of full employment, high productivity and growth, and low inflation.

Although each of these goals can be discussed in isolation, they are ineluctably intertwined. For example, dependence on foreign oil not only raises the stakes for control in the Middle East but also makes the economy more vulnerable to inflationary price shocks—a factor that in turn threatens economic growth and stability. Recognizing these linkages, let us focus first on national energy and security, a discussion that leads naturally to examining other policy goals.

ENERGY POLICY

The Arab oil embargo of 1973-74 was a rude awakening for a nation that since the end of World War II had been steadily building up its industrial infrastructure, transportation systems, and electricity sys-

71

tems on the foundation of low-priced and plentiful petroleum supplies. In 1948, oil and natural gas supplied 47 percent of America's energy needs, and King Coal accounted for over 76 percent of total fuel consumption in the electric utility sector.[1] By 1965, however, U.S. reliance on oil and gas had increased to 74 percent of total energy needs, and the utility industry had switched to oil and gas to meet over 33 percent of its fuel needs.[2]

The steadily increasing dependence on petroleum was first fed primarily by domestic production in Texas, Oklahoma, California, and other petroleum-rich states. By the late 1960s, their derricks steadily pumped out about 8 million barrels of oil a day and 20 million cubic feet of natural gas.[3]

During these years, though, discovery of new domestic petroleum reserves lagged far behind the growth in domestic consumption; U.S. oil production peaked in 1970, but demand still rose. To satiate its appetite for petroleum, America had to look beyond its national boundaries. With foreign oil selling at an average cost of some $2 per barrel, increasing imports appeared to be a good idea.[4] And increase our imports we did, from 3.4 million barrels per day (mbd) in 1970 to 6.3 mbd in 1973—an 83 percent increase.[5]

The lion's share of these imports came from the member states of the Organization of Petroleum Exporting Countries—the OPEC cartel. By 1973 OPEC imports had reached 3 mbd, roughly half of all petroleum imports and one-fourth of total U.S. oil consumption.[6] Of OPEC imports, the largest share of the 3-mbd dependence came from Arab nations in the Middle East, which provided nearly 1 mbd.[7] That represented 15 percent of all imports and three-fifths of oil consumption in the utility industry, which by 1973 was topping 1.5 mbd. Thus, the stage was set for a series of unprecedented events in the oil markets, triggered by the Yom Kippur War between Egypt and Israel.

In late October of 1973, as an uneasy truce settled over that war, the world's third largest oil producer, Saudi Arabia, joined with Libya,

1. U.S. Department of Energy, Energy Information Administration, *Annual Report to Congress, 1978* (Washington, D.C.).

2. *Edison Electric Institute Statistical Yearbook*, (New York: Edison Electric Institute).

3. *1982 Annual Energy Review* and U.S. Department of Energy, Energy Information Administration, *Natural Gas Annuals* (Washington, D.C.).

4. *The Royal Dutch/Shell Information Handbook 1982–83* (London, 1983), p. 126.

5. *1982 Annual Energy Review.*

6. *Energy Policy*, 2d ed. (Washington, D.C.: Congressional Quarterly, Inc., 1981), p. 5.

7. *1982 Annual Energy Review.*

Kuwait, Qatar, Bahrain, and Dubai to declare a total embargo of oil exports to the United States as retaliation for its support of Israel. Shortly thereafter, the Shah of Iran pressed to more than double the price of oil, and these price hikes were subsequently ratified by the OPEC cartel. The rest, as the saying goes, is history.

The embargo and subsequent price shocks created long lines at the gas station, truckers' strikes, a federally mandated speed limit, a government-controlled thermostat, and cutbacks in auto production, among other things. The events of 1973 also created an awareness of a need for what America had hitherto lacked, namely, a coordinated and well-defined national energy policy. In November of that year, President Nixon set the major goal of that policy when he remarked: "Let us set as our national goal . . . that by the end of this decade we will have developed the potential to meet our own energy needs without depending on any foreign source."[8]

Complete energy independence within a decade quickly proved, however, to be a chimera. Indeed, even as the Nixon and Ford administrations were mandating the Federal Energy Administration to get "Project Independence" off the ground, the United States was becoming even more dependent on foreign oil. By 1977, U.S. imports of petroleum climbed to a record high of 8.8 mbd, and OPEC oil accounted for 70 percent of that total.[9] Meanwhile, despite several attempts by the federal government to force it to convert a large portion of its capacity to coal, the utility industry continued to consume oil at a rate of over 1 million barrels per day.[10]

Recognizing this continued reliance on foreign oil and the apparent failure of Project Independence, in 1977 President Carter established a new set of energy goals embodied in his National Energy Plan. Backing away from both autarky and the Nixon 1980 deadline, the new energy plan set as a major goal the reduction of oil imports to 7 million barrels a day by 1985. At the same time, the plan established a Strategic Petroleum Reserve (proposed by the Ford administration), which would be filled with what was estimated to be a ten-month supply, or 1 billion barrels.

Shortly thereafter, recognizing both the importance of the electric utility industry in meeting the goals of the National Energy Plan and

8. President Nixon's speech to the public, November 7, 1973.
9. *1982 Annual Energy Review*.
10. Ibid.

the growing financial constraints of that industry in its first decade of rate suppression, the Carter administration also initiated legislation in the Congress to financially assist, and in some cases force, utilities to reduce their petroleum consumption. This "oil backout bill"[11] took dead aim at 1 million barrels per day of oil and natural gas that the industry was capable of economically reducing; but with a price tag to the taxpayers of some $10 billion dollars, the bill died in Congress.[12]

Today, while America is less susceptible to an oil supply interruption than it was in 1973, it is still heavily dependent on foreign oil. Our imports averaged 4.3 mbd in 1982, and as the economy picks up steam at a moderate rate, these imports are projected to rise to 6.1 mbd by 1985.[13]

THE UTILITY INDUSTRY, NATIONAL ENERGY POLICY, AND NATIONAL SECURITY

Where does the electric utility industry fit in the current U.S. energy policy picture? Despite a slackening in energy demand due to conservation and slower economic growth, the industry continues to be the same position it was in when the 1973-74 embargo struck. That is, it remains the single largest stationary consumer of petroleum in the nation and remains the single largest target for the economic reduction of petroleum consumption.

In 1982 the industry consumed 680,000 barrels of oil per day and another 1.4 million equivalent barrels of natural gas.[14] This utility use of oil and gas constitutes roughly half our total net petroleum

11. President Carter's message to Congress, April 20, 1977.

12. The bill was introduced in March 1980 and consisted of two parts. Phase I required the conversion of 21,000 megawatts of oil-burning capacity to coal by 1985, affected plants primarily in the Northeast, and offered federal assistance to utilities undertaking such conversions. Phase II was a voluntary program which intended to displace another 600,000 barrels of oil by 1990.

13. U.S. Department of Energy, Office of Electrical Systems, "Staff Analysis of the Energy and Economic Impacts of the President's Program for Reducing Oil and Gas Consumption in the Utility Sector" (Washington, D.C., April 21, 1980), pp. 1 and 10.

14. Figures are from the *Monthly Energy Review* (Washington, D.C.: U.S. Department of Energy, Energy Information Administration, DOE/EIA–0035. December 1983/2: 73. Note that many analysts believe that because of economic recession, recent statistics understate utilities' dependence on oil.

imports.[15] Most such utility oil and gas use can be economically eliminated through the options described in detail in Chapter 3— namely, coal conversion, new construction to allow retirement of usable but economically obsolete petroleum plants, conservation, and other petroleum-saving projects.

However, as Chapter 3 demonstrated in its discussion of the fuel penalty, the utility industry has resisted pursuing these economic options because from the standpoint of its firms—rather than that of the national welfare—it is simply unprofitable or financially infeasible to do so. Today, over 8,000 megawatts of coal-capable capacity remain to be converted to coal. At the same time, an additional 196,000 megawatts of oil- and gas-fired plants can be economically displaced by nonpetroleum sources (roughly three-fourths of this capacity is steam-fired and hence predominantly baseload).[16] For a number of reasons, such heavy utility reliance on oil and gas is likely to continue.

First, as the American economy continues its forecast recovery, utility petroleum consumption has begun to and will continue to increase as those plants now called on for only part of their generating capacity are pressed into fuller service. Second, this effect of economic recovery on utility petroleum use will be augmented by the effect of population expansion and other factors. Again, because utilities are holding their most expensive capacity in reserve, it is those oil- and gas-fired plants that will be used to meet increased demand. A strategy of capital minimization makes it unlikely that utilities will undertake new construction projects instead.

Thus, the rate-suppression/capital-minimization syndrome coupled with economic growth will probably carry us further from, rather than nearer to, our national energy-policy goals. The costs of not meeting the goal of import reductions are by now well-known. The probability of a major military conflict over the Middle East is generally thought to rise with U.S. import dependence. As a potential dispute with either hostile Arab nations and/or the Soviet Union threatens to prevent Persian Gulf oil from flowing, U.S. military spending and activity within the area increases.

15. The actual figure is 49.9 percent. This can be derived from the *Monthly Energy Review* (December 1983/2): 33, 73, and back cover.
16. Department of Energy spokesperson.

Today we are already spending over $5 billion per year on foreign aid and on maintenance of a military presence in the Middle East, and the Reagan administration continues to press for more and more funds for the region.[17] At the same time, some 300,000 troops are designated to be assigned to the U.S. Central Command (formerly known as the Rapid Deployment Task Force) if it were activated. Those troops spend a fair amount of time practicing missions geared to the Middle East, an area of possible deployment.[18]

Meanwhile, we continue to fill our Strategic Petroleum Reserve. This insurance policy against an import cutoff will cost roughly $15 billion to top off.[19] The SPR reached its half-way mark in December 1983, and at its current fill rate, it will reach its ultimate goal of 750 million barrels in early 1991.

ECONOMIC POLICY

A reduction in petroleum import dependence is also highly correlated with economic policy goals. Consider, for example, inflation. America's, and indeed the world's, heavy dependence on foreign oil made it vulnerable to the series of oil price shocks during the 1970s. Petroleum price hikes, notably the fourfold leap in 1974 and the twofold leap in the late 1970s, were largely responsible for double-digit inflation rates experienced in that decade.

While the early 1980s have seen a softening of oil prices (and not coincidentally, a reduction in inflation), continued heavy reliance on imports leaves us vulnerable to the inflationary pressure that would inevitably result from a tightening of the oil markets—and many analysts believe the oil markets must eventually tighten.

Rate suppression also poses a threat to economic growth via the reliability penalty. Many analysts now agree that a fairly well-defined relationship exists between economic growth as measured by the gross national product (GNP) and growth in electricity demand. Between 1960 and 1973, average annual electricity demand grew 1.7 times faster than GNP. This means that for every 1 percent increase in the GNP, electricity was growing at a rate of 1.7 percent.

17. *Congressional Quarterly,* 5th ed., Washington, D.C., p. 74.
18. Defense Department spokesperson.
19. *Strategic Petroleum Reserve Annual Report* (Washington, D.C.: U.S. Government Printing Office, 1984).

Since 1973 conservation has brought that ratio down somewhat, but electricity demand has still grown 1.2 times as fast as GNP; that is, a 1 percent growth in the GNP is accompanied by at least a 1.2 percent growth in electricity demand. This link between GNP and electricity demand has continued, then, even as the link between nonelectric energy demand and GNP growth has been decoupled. Indeed, while total nonelectric energy demand grew at about 0.8 times GNP during the 1960–73 period, that figure has actually declined slightly in the postembargo era.[20] A major reason for this decline—and for the continued growth in electricity demand—is, of course, that residents, businesses, and industries are switching from more expensive petroleum to electricity. This electrification of the economy is evident in the fact that in 1960 one-fourth of all the energy used in America went into generating electricity; today that figure is one-third.[21] At the same time, electricity's share of the total U.S. energy consumption has risen from 23 percent in 1972 to 34 percent today.[22]

Should the link betwen GNP and electricity demand hold over the next several decades, the problem the rate-suppression/capital-minimization syndrome poses is this: If electricity supply is constrained from growing, any increase in demand will have to go unmet. (According to the Department of Energy, electricity demand can be expected to grow at a rate at least equal to the growth of the nation's economy through the remainder of this century.)[23] Such an occurrence might preclude sustained economic recovery. In the worst-case scenario, insufficient electricity capacity will be a major obstacle to GNP growth and will therefore affect employment opportunities and prevent a rise in real income and the overall prosperity that economic growth would bring.

To assess the likelihood of such a scenario consider the following. Once again, assuming that demand for electricity will grow at the moderate rate of 3 percent a year and allowing for a 20 percent reserve margin, the DOE figures that the United States must be able to supply 901 gigawatts of electricity by the year 2000. As of 1981, U.S. generating capability was 572 gigawatts. Thus, an additional

20. *The Future of Electric Power* (Washington, D.C.: U.S. Department of Energy, Office of Policy, Planning, and Analysis, June 1983), p. ES-4.

21. U.S. Committee for Energy Awareness, 'The Electrical Age: Rebirth or Retreat?'' (Washington, D.C.: U.S. Committee for Energy Awareness, 1983 booklet), p. 6.

22. U.S. Committee for Energy Awareness, "The Electrical Age," p. 5.

23. *Future of Electric Power*, p. ES-5.

329 gigawatts is required by 2000. By subtracting the capacity of plants expected to be retired in the coming fourteen years and the capacity lost as power plants age and become less available for service, the DOE finds that 438 gigawatts of new capacity will be needed. In other words, if electricity demand grows at a moderate rate, we will have to increase our capacity by approximately one-half by the turn of the century. Moreover, the total cumulative capital investment required by the electric utility industry through the year 2000 is approximately $1 trillion. By comparison, the total existing asset base of the electric power industry (both public and private) in 1981 was about $300 billion. Thus, the investment required at a 3 percent rate of load growth through 2000 will be roughly three times as great as the utility investment already in place (in nominal terms).[24]

The electric utility industry's capital minimization strategy—its only viable response to rate suppression—obviously is not conducive to preparing to meet that need. The North American Electric Reliability Council projects that supply will fall short in 1993 if demand grows at 3 percent a year. If demand grows faster, say at 4 percent a year, supply will be inadequate as early as 1990. Even if utilities continue to use uneconomic oil and natural gas plants in an effort to meet demand, they will only postpone demand shortfalls by about five years. Further, because these figures are national averages and regional supply and demand are not homogeneous, some areas of the country could be hit by supply shortfalls before that time.

Rate suppression is likely to have important microeconomic effects centering on productivity and its relationship to inflation and real income at the individual business firm level. Higher productivity makes it possible to produce more goods and services with the same amounts of labor, capital, and natural resources. Because high productivity means that goods are produced more efficiently, the prices of those goods is kept low, and inflation is thereby held down. Because people can afford to buy more when prices are low, real income rises.

Many of today's business investment opportunities that might lead to higher productivity are, however, electricity-intensive. Such productivity-enhancing innovations range from computers, telecommunications systems, word processors, and robotics to advanced electromechanical devices and electronic vehicles. Part of the cost advantage Japanese steelmakers enjoy over their American counter-

24. *Future of Electric Power*, p. ES–15.

parts is due to the adoption of electric-arc furnaces, which greatly reduce ore-handling costs, economize on coal resources, and provide a more precise method of metal fabrication. Any successful modernization of the American steel industry will include introduction of these more productive and efficient—though electricity-intensive—furnaces. Similarly, the renaissance of the auto industry rests in large part on time- and labor-saving devices like robots, which feed on electricity. U.S. plastic manufacturers are turning to electrically heated injection-molding machines to stay one step ahead of the competition, just as textile, paper, and grain companies are turning to microwave technology for heating and drying applications.

But if business executives perceive electricity supplies as becoming more and more expensive (due to the fuel and cost of capital penalties) and in shorter and shorter supply (via the reliability penalty), they may very well choose to forgo undertaking such investments.

The specter of shortages and higher prices may also affect decisions on plant location, capacity expansion, and power supply. Given the tenuous supply situation in California, for example, some high-tech companies in Silicon Valley may choose to migrate to, say, New Mexico, where both electricity supply and the regulatory climate are much more favorable. By the same token, aluminum producers in the Pacific Northwest may forgo domestic expansion in favor of building new production facilities abroad where electricity is cheaper. Concern over potential shortages may even force some companies to build their own generating capacities, even though doing so will drain capital from more productive forms of investment and test the limits of managerial competence.

In summary, the rate-suppression/capital-minimization syndrome threatens a wide range of national energy, security, and economic policy goals. In some cases, the costs of failing to meet these goals are fairly obvious; in other cases, less so.

Will an electricity supply shortage help to derail our economy as it spurs inflation, constrains our industry, and damages productivity? Will the specter of shortages reduce the rate of productivity-enhancing investment and force industries to relocate? Will our international economic standing be irreparably crippled by the short-sightedness of our energy planners as other nations surge ahead? These are questions that only time will answer, but such questions must be considered in the electric utility policy debate.

7 RATE SUPPRESSION AND CONSUMERS' ELECTRICITY BILLS

The greatest irony of the rate-suppression/capital-minimization syndrome is that the ostensible beneficiaries of rate suppression—electricity consumers—are likely to be its biggest losers. The losses to consumers will come in the form of higher rates for less reliable service. Higher rates will result from the fuel and cost-of-capital penalties imposed by rate suppression, while less reliable service will result directly from the reliability penalty. By and large, consumers will not fully bear these costs until it is too late to do anything to avoid the consequences of rate suppression. Understanding why this is so requires an awareness of the trade-off between the short-run benefits of rate suppression and its longer-run costs.

This chapter presents the results of a study on the costs and benefits of rate suppression that I conducted for the Department of Energy under the auspices of the Energy and Environmental Policy Center at Harvard University.[1] The aim of that study was to forecast future electricity rates and system reliability under rate suppression. The results of the study were clear: Under plausible assumptions about fuel prices and energy demand growth, both rates and reliability will suffer if rate suppression continues.

1. Peter Navarro, "Long Term Consumer Impacts of Electricity Rate Regulatory Policies" (prepared for U.S. Department of Energy, Washington, D.C., January 1983).

81

THE SHORT-VERSUS THE LONGER-RUN EFFECTS

In the short run, PUC regulation may be thought of as a zero-sum game between electricity consumers and utility shareholders. Every dollar of a rate increase that the PUC refuses to grant the utility represents a dollar off consumers' electricity bills. In this time frame, consumers are clearly better off under rate suppression; after all, rate suppression by definition means that rates are being held below the market cost of generating electricity.

As we have seen in the preceding chapters, however, PUC regulation does not take place in the freeze-frame of a single rate case. Utility executives base their investment and operating strategies not just on the outcome of their most recent rate case but also on the regulatory treatment they expect to receive in the future.

We have also seen that in the presence of rate suppression, utility executives are likely to underinvest in projects that are necessary to keep the lights on and to keep electricity prices as low as possible. This underinvestment in turn creates the fuel, cost-of-capital, and reliability penalties. The trade-off of rate suppression, then, is that in the short run, rates are lower than they otherwise would be because the PUC fails to give the utility the opportunity to earn its market cost of capital and fully recover its expenses. In the longer run, however, even if the PUC continues to hold rates below the utility's market cost of capital, rates are higher than they would have been without rate suppression. This is so because the fuel and cost-of-capital penalties drive the utility's expenses higher than they must otherwise be.

This trade-off of rate suppression is illustrated in Figure 7–1, which shows over time the general profiles of electricity rates under two alternative regulatory futures. The dotted line indicates what electricity rates would be under rate suppression; the solid line plots electricity rates under "capital attraction" (whereby the utility is allowed to earn its market cost of capital). Note that in the figure the dotted line starts below the solid line, indicating lower rates in the short run. But because the slope of the dotted line is steeper than that of the solid line, sometime in the future there is a crossover point after which the price of electricity is actually higher under rate suppression.

The figure poses an interesting question: Are consumers better off paying rates that follow the dotted line of rate suppression or the solid

Figure 7–1. Time Profile of Electricity Rates in Two Regulatory Regimes.

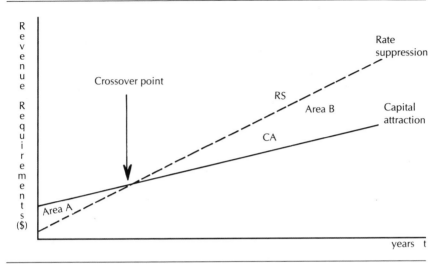

Source: Peter Navarro, of the Harvard University Energy and Environmental Policy Center, *Long Term Consumer Impacts of Electricity Rate Regulatory Policies*, (prepared for the U.S. Department of Energy, January 1983).

line of capital attraction? In other words, is it to their benefit to pay lower rates now but higher rates later (rate suppression) or to pay slightly higher rates now so that rates will be lower in the future (capital attraction)?

Figure 7-1 can be used to derive an answer to that question. Area *A* represents the dollar value of the *benefits* of rate suppression, and Area *B* represents the extra *costs* of rate suppression. By comparing these two areas, we can ascertain whether the costs of rate suppression outweigh the benefits, or vice versa. Before drawing a comparison, however, we must make adjustments to take into account the time value of money. That is, we must take into account the fact that because of the opportunity to earn interest on one's money, a dollar today is worth more than a dollar a year from today.[2] Financial experts make such adjustments by using net present value discounting. This financial tool can convert a stream of numbers over time into a

2. For example, if I have a dollar today, I can invest it in a money market and earn, say, 10 percent, making my dollar worth $1.10 next year.

single number that represents the value of that stream in today's dollars.[3]

To see how this tool works, suppose that the benefits of rate suppression will be $20 in the first year, $10 in the second year, and zero dollars in the third year (the crossover point). At an interest rate of 10 percent per year, the net present value of these benefits will be roughly $26.[4] On the other hand, suppose the costs of rate suppression will be $10 per year in the fourth year, $20 in the fifth year, and $30 in the sixth year. At an interest rate of 10 percent, the net present value of these costs will be roughly $40.[5] Thus, in this case, the dollar value of Area A (the benefits) would be $14 less than the dollar value of Area B (the costs), which means that consumers would be worse off in the long run.

THE DOE STUDY

To root this theory of the dynamics of rate suppression in reality, I forecast future electricity rates and system reliabilities for a representative sample of the nation's utilities using a ratemaking model that is in wide use among PUCs. The six utilities in the sample were selected to ensure variety in load growth, in the percentage of petroleum in the generation mix, and in regional location—the three characteristics most important in determining the magnitude of the regulatory penalties. The greater a utility's load growth, for instance, the more it will need additional sources of electricity. If the utility builds new plants to meet that growth, the cost-of-capital penalty will be more severe. If it instead purchases power at a cost above what its generating costs would be, the fuel penalty will rise. And if those additional sources of power are unavailable, the reliability penalty will increase. Similarly, the greater a utility's dependence on petroleum-fired power plants, the greater its potential for reducing its petroleum consumption. Thus, the fuel penalty is higher for a utility that relies more heavily on petroleum power plants.

The utilities included here are representative in the sense that they reflect different combinations of conditions typical of the industry as

3. For discussion of this technique, see, for example, Eugene F. Brigham, *Fundamentals of Financial Management* (New York: Dryden Press, 1983).
4. The calculation is $20/1.10 + 10/(1.10)^2 = \$26.45$.
5. The calculation is $10/(1.10)^4 + 30/(1.10)^5 = \$39.80$.

a whole. They come from six major regions of the country—New England, the Southeast, the Southwest, the Midwest, the Rocky Mountains, and the Pacific Coast. Their forecast load growths range from 1.5 percent to 4.0 percent a year, and their petroleum dependence ranges from zero to 60 percent. (Because of the political sensitivity of the rate-suppression issue with respect to ratepayers and PUCs, all of the participating utilities requested anonymity.)

Each of the six utilities was asked to forecast the investment program it would pursue in response to two different hypothetical regulatory climates.[6] The rate-suppressive regime was defined as a regulatory climate in which the utility could expect to earn a real (inflation-adjusted) return on common equity of 4 percent, which is three percentage points less than the 7 percent real return on equity utilities needed to meet their estimated market cost of capital in the last decade. As Chapter 2 indicated, the 4 percent rate of return approximates the real return the utility industry has obtained since the Arab oil embargo. The capital attraction regime was defined as a regulatory climate in which the utility would be allowed to earn its full market cost of capital, a 7 percent real rate of return.

THE STUDY'S RESULTS

When faced with the rate-suppression regime, each utility forecast that it would continue its current strategy of holding capital expenditures down as low as possible. But when faced with the regulatory-reform or capital-attraction scenario, they all forecast robust programs of capital expansion. A discussion of some of the representative utilities' alternative investment and operating strategies sheds further light on the dynamics of the rate-suppression/capital-minimization syndrome.

In the capital-attraction scenario, the *New England* utility invested a total of $9.9 billion over the forecast period (to the year 2000). During the 1980s it converted over 800 megawatts of existing oil capacity to coal, and it finished on schedule the construction of a large nuclear plant. During the 1990s it also built four 600-megawatt coal

---

6. The utilities' forecasts were generated by their own engineering and financial models, which find the investment strategy that minimizes ratepayer costs subject to financial constraints. Each forecast was carefully checked for plausibility.

plants (in which it retained two-thirds ownership) to meet projected load growth, and it retired aging plants on schedule. Reliance on purchased power was limited to small transactions with other members of its power pool and comprised a negligible portion of its peak demand.

In contrast, under the rate-suppression scenario, the New England utility spent only $4.1 billion. It converted less than 200 megawatts of oil capacity to coal and sold half of its share in the nuclear plant under construction in order to finance the plant's completion (rather than borrowing or issuing stock). To meet load during the 1980s, it began to reduce its sales of electricity to outside customers, and by the end of the 1990s it was a net purchaser, buying power equivalent to roughly 175 megawatts of capacity, or 3 percent of its peak load. At the same time, it retired none of its existing capacity.

Under the capital-attraction scenario, the *Midwest* utility completed with no delay during the 1980s several large nuclear plants that were under construction. During the 1990s four additional coal units (totaling over 2,000 megawatts) were built, and the company also assumed a 75 percent share of two additional 1,100-megawatt nuclear units coming on line at the turn of the century. Finally, an intermediate-load ("cycling") coal plant was built in the early 1990s, and all plants were retired on schedule.

Under the rate-suppression scenario, two-thirds of the new nuclear capacity was delayed four years, so that the completion date of the last unit was pushed from 1986 to 1990. No further construction was undertaken, nor was any existing plant retired, except for one small plant retired in both scenarios. To meet load, the utility more than doubled its purchased power and increased the use of its existing oil and natural gas capacity. Over twice as much oil and three times as much gas were consumed than in the capital-attraction scenario.

The *Southwest* utility steadily added over 5,000 megawatts of new coal capacity in 600-megawatt increments between 1982 and 1997 and added a similar amount between 1998 and 2009 in the capital-attraction scenario. Each of the plants was built before it was needed for load growth and was used to displace natural gas consumption. This approach allowed the utility to maintain a comfortable reserve margin in excess of 20 percent over the period.

In the second scenario, the utility built 2,000 megawatts less coal capacity in the time frame 1982–97, solely to meet load. At the same time, its existing oil and gas capacity was extended well beyond its planned service life. By 1998 the utility was forced to undertake the construction of 6,000 megawatts of new coal capacity through the year 2009 to replace its aging plants. However, its reserve margin dropped from over 20 percent to 13 percent between 1982 and 1990 and to a perilous 9.6 percent by the year 2000.

The *Pacific Coast* utility, under the capital-attraction scenario, adopted a three-pronged investment strategy to reduce its oil use. In the mid-1980s it purchased a share of a large coal plant under construction. At the same time, it participated as a joint owner in a major coal project, with capacity coming on line in the early 1990s. Finally, it built additional transmission lines to purchase power at favorable contract prices to help meet load in the 1990s. All three of these projects were designed to reduce oil consumption through coal displacement and economy purchases.

Under the assumption that the regulatory environment was rate-suppressive, none of the three projects was undertaken. Instead, the retirement of over 2,000 megawatts of natural gas and oil capacity was deferred.

The pattern of investment for the *Rocky Mountain* and *Southeast* utilities is similar. Table 7–1 summarizes the utilities' projected capital expenditures and expenses for fuel and purchased power for the two sets of investment and operating strategies. It is clear that each utility's choices of inputs differ widely for the two alternative scenarios. Under the capital-attraction scenario, when the utility expects to earn its cost of capital, it chooses a considerably larger capital budget and a correspondingly smaller level of fuel and purchased power expenses than under the rate-suppression regime.

Consider, for example, the New England utility's choices. In the capital-attraction scenario, it sets a $9.9 billion capital budget and spends $29.9 billion on fuel and purchased power. Under rate suppression it invests only $4.1 billion but spends more than $43.2 billion on fuel and purchased power. Similarly, the Pacific Coast utility chooses a $22.1 billion capital budget and spends $77.2 on fuel and purchased power in the capital-attraction scenario, but given rate suppression, it invests only $12.9 billion and spends $95.3 billion on fuel and purchased power.

Only the Southwest utility invests more under rate suppression, despite the fact that this utility actually winds up with an additional 2,000 megawatts more capacity in the capital-attraction scenario. The higher capital budget under rate suppression in large part reflects the

Table 7–1.   Utility Spending under Two Hypothetical Scenarios.

Representative Utility	Capital Attraction		Rate Suppression	
	Capital Expenditures	Fuel and Purchased- Power Expenses	Capital Expenditures	Fuel and Purchased- Power Expenses
New England	$ 9.9	$ 29.9	$ 4.1	$ 43.2
Midwest	40.6	110.4	23.9	139.4
Southwest	62.8	152.1	64.8	201.0
Southeast	30.5	107.8	8.9	133.6
Pacific Coast	22.1	77.2	12.9	95.3
Rocky Mountain	7.6	35.6	4.8	45.4

Note: Fuel and purchased power expenses were calculated under rising fuel price assumptions, explained in the text.

higher (nominal) capital costs of the 6,000 megawatts it waits until the year 1998 to build. And because under rate suppression the utility forgoes economic gas displacement before 1998, its fuel and purchased-power expenses are higher under rate suppression than under capital attraction ($201.0 billion compared with $152.1 billion).

Table 7–1 also provides supportive evidence for the reverse AJ effect discussed in Chapter 2. This effect predicts that as a regulated company's expected return on capital declines, so too will its use of capital in the production process. However, neither the AJ literature nor Table 7–1 answers the question, Which investment strategy will minimize costs to ratepayers over time?

To answer that question, I used a ratemaking model in wide use among the PUCs (the regulatory analysis model) to calculate the six utilities' annual electricity rates for the next two decades. I made separate sets of calculations for the two investment strategies and used two different assumptions about fuel prices. The rising-fuel-price case assumed a 2 percent real annual increase in the prices of oil and natural gas (to account for deregulation, the price for natural gas is assumed to rise only after 1985) and a 1 percent real annual increase in the price of coal. These assumptions are in line with forecasts of the Department of Energy, the Electric Power Research Institute, and other observers. The stable-fuel-price case, included to allay fears that the results might be driven primarily by rising fuel prices, assumed *no* increase in real fuel prices. I also calculated reserve margins.

Table 7–2.   Costs to Ratepayers of Rate Suppression.

Representative Utility	Assuming Rising Fuel Costs		Assuming Stable Fuel Costs	
	Net Present Value of Benefits (millions)	Internal Rate of Return	Net Present Value of Benefits (millions)	Internal Rate of Return
New England	$1,289	40%	$ 513	28%
Midwest	242	16	-279	11
Southwest	2,302	36	995	26
Southeast	2,840	38	1,555	29
Pacific Coast	1,530	20	3	14
Rocky Mountain	607	40	695	41

Source: Peter Navarro, of the Harvard University Energy and Environmental Center, *Long Term Consumer Impacts of Electricity Rate Regulation Policies*, (prepared for the U.S. Department of Energy, January 1983).

As expected, under rate suppression, rates were lower in the early 1980s for both the rising and the stable-fuel-price cases. Then, as higher fuel costs and carrying charges accumulated, rates eventually crossed over for both cases, typically during the mid-1980s. From that point on, electricity prices were consistently higher—yet the rate-suppressed utilities were still earning a lower return on investment. The gap in electricity rates widened steadily, so that by the year 2000 rates were dramatically higher under rate suppression than under a capital-attraction regime. In the rising-fuel-price case, electric bills to Pacific Coast utility customers were 11 percent higher; for Southeast utility ratepayers, they were 33 percent higher.

To compare these two possible futures of electricity prices, I used the net present value discounting procedure described earlier.[7] The results are reported in Table 7-2, which catalogs the net present value of the costs of rate suppression under the two alternative fuel-price assumptions. The table also shows an internal rate of return (IRR), which equates the net present value of the two electricity rate streams. This IRR is equivalent to what the consumers' discount rate would have to be in order for them to be indifferent to lower rates now (under rate suppression) as opposed to lower rates later (under capital

7. The net present value of benefits is calculated by assuming a real discount rate of 6 percent. This means that at an inflation rate of, say, 8 percent, the discount rate would be 14 percent.

attraction). If the IRR is very high—beyond the plausible range of the ratepayers' discount rate—then it provides additional evidence that consumers are indeed better off under capital attraction (and conversely for rate suppression).

The IRR is also a measure of the return on consumers' investment in higher rates in the short run. That is, when the consumer pays higher rates in the short run, he or she is in one sense providing the utility with not only the incentive but also the financial resources to undertake a more economical investment and operating strategy. The return on the ratepayer's investment comes in the form of rates that are lower than they otherwise would be later. The rate of return is what ratepayers would earn on the investment by paying slightly higher rates in the earlier years.

In a scenario of moderately rising fuel prices, the benefits to be gained from capital attraction are startling, ranging from $242 million for the Midwest utility to $2.8 billion for the Southeast utility. Moreover, these sums translate into whopping double-digit internal rates of return. For example, the $1.3 billion that the New England utility's ratepayers would save amounts to an annual return for them of 40 percent on average over the forecast period. Indeed, the ratepayers of four of the six utilities would realize rates of return above 35 percent—roughly three times the annual return on the stock market over the last decade and more than twice the yield of money market funds.

What happens to these whopping benefits and investment returns when fuel prices are assumed to be stable? In particular, does the fuel penalty shrink to the point where rate suppression becomes worthwhile for consumers? The answer is a surprising no. For four of the six utilities (the same four that had especially high rates of return when fuel prices increased), ratepayer benefits still range from the hundreds of millions to billions of dollars, and ratepayer returns are above 25 percent. The New England utility, for example, saves its ratepayers $513 million for a return of 28 percent, while Rocky Mountain's return to ratepayers hits 41 percent. For only two utilities does the return fall into the range where other kinds of investments—in stocks, bonds, and money market—might be competitive.

Not unexpectedly, the weakest case turns out to be the Midwest utility, which has the lowest rate of oil consumption and hence the smallest fuel penalty. Its ratepayers actually *lose* $279 million (in a present-value sense) under an improved regulatory climate and with steady fuel prices, although they still earn a positive rate of return of

11 percent. Slightly more robust is the Pacific Coast utility, with savings of a scant $3 million and a modest but respectable 14 percent rate of return.

The story is not yet complete, however, because we still have to measure the reliability penalty. Here I found dangerously low reserve margins for four of the six utilities, with the most perilous situation occurring in the Midwest utility. Under rate suppression, this utility's reserve margin plunged from 23 percent to a razor-thin 5 percent by the year 2000—well below the 15 percent to 20 percent a utility needs to ensure uninterrupted service. Similarly, the reserve margin of the Southwest utility fell to 8 percent.

The bottom line, then, is that in return for the luxury of lower rates for a few short years in the 1980s, all six utilities' customers would pay dramatically higher rates over many years or would have far less reliable service or both.[8] An alternative electricity future is offered by the U.S. Department of Energy's Policy Project report:

Increased rates to improve the financial condition of the industry and thereby encourage construction would involve increases in electric prices averaging only five to six percent. These increased costs would be more than offset by savings which yield a rate of return to consumers ranging between sixteen and forty percent over the long term. Accordingly, consumers would be well served by 'investing' in the improved financial performance of their utility company. Their investment in near-term electric price increases would be handsomely compensated by longer-term rate reductions.[9]

More broadly, analysis of this representative sample of utilities points to a precarious and expensive future for consumers if the current trend toward rate suppression is not reversed. This appears to be true even if petroleum prices do not resume their rapid rise. To avert this future, we must reduce and, where possible, eliminate the underlying causes of rate suppression.

The next chapter identifies those causes within the context of the political, institutional, and ideological forces bearing down on the PUCs. The final chapter lays out a policy blueprint to counter these forces and to reduce both the causes and effects of rate suppression.

8. The hard-to-qualify social and economic costs of these falling reserve margins and associated shortages were necessarily ignored in the ratepayer-cost calculation. Thus, the costs to ratepayers presented here understate—possibly to a great degree—the true costs of rate suppression.

9. *The Future of Electric Power in America* (Washington, D.C.: U.S. Department of Energy, Office of Policy, Planning and Analysis, June 1983), p. ES–14.

IV SEEKING AN ALTERNATIVE ELECTRICITY FUTURE

Political Pressure	Government Failure	Ideological Goals

8 THE POLITICS OF RATE SUPPRESSION

The key to understanding why rate suppression occurs lies in an examination of the political, institutional, and ideological forces that regularly buffet the nation's PUCs. In a nutshell, political pressures force PUCs to suppress rates, institutional pressures prevent PUCs from raising rates as fast as inflation, and in an era of rapidly rising energy and capital costs, rate suppression is a convenient device to achieve several ideological goals. This chapter uses three models of regulatory behavior to explain and then test the potential importance of these forces.

POLITICAL CAPTURE

According to Nobel Laureate and Chicago economist George Stigler, government regulatory agencies are designed by and operate primarily for the benefit of powerful special interests at the expense of less powerful interests.[1] According to this Stiglerian capture model, natural gas price controls, for example, exist to redistribute income from gas producers to gas consumers, and airline regulations of previous

1. George J. Stigler, "The Economic Theory of Regulation," *Bell Journal of Economics* (Spring 1971): 3.

decades existed to feather the nests of the major airlines at the expense of air travelers.

In the case of electric utility regulation, the two major interest groups are ratepayers and utility shareholders. Seen through the lens of the capture theory, PUC regulation is merely the vehicle for a distributional struggle between these two warring factions: For any given rate case, every dollar of rate relief the PUC awards the utility means a dollar out of consumers' pockets over the short term. The presence of rate suppression, then, simply indicates that ratepayers have captured the PUCs. There are several reasons why this might be so.

First, electricity consumers vastly outnumber utility shareholders. Of course, this numerical superiority does not guarantee political success, for many numerically large groups in America—the poor and the uneducated, for example—have very little political power. As economist Mancur Olson and political scientist James Q. Wilson have explained, many large groups like consumers and the poor are often unorganized and weak because the costs that special interests impose on them are diffuse while the benefits to the special interests are very concentrated.[2]

When a utility files for a $100 million rate hike, for instance, a relatively small number of shareholders stand to win or lose a substantial part of their investment earnings. On the other hand, the numerically larger group of consumers has stood to win or lose a few more cents or dollars on their monthly bills. This asymmetry has given utilities, on behalf of their shareowners, great incentive—and ratepayers very little—to organize and lobby the PUCs.

The rapid increases in electricity prices over the past decade, however, have dramatically raised the stakes in the PUC ratemaking game. It's no longer a matter of a few cents or dollars more; consumers have seen their bills double and triple. Not surprisingly, consumers have responded to these rate hikes with increased organization and political activity. As part of a more general trend toward consumer activism, electricity utility consumers have become much more adept at flexing their political muscle against what has traditionally been a well-heeled and powerful utility lobby.

2. Mancur Olson, *The Logic of Collective Action: Public Goods and the Theory of Groups* (New York: Harvard University Press and Schocken Books, 1965); James Q. Wilson, "The Politics of Regulation," in *Social Responsibility and the Business Predicament*, James W. McKie, ed. (Washington, D.C.: Brookings Institution, 1974).

This trend toward consumer power has paralleled the increased incidence of rate suppression. In this regard, sharply rising energy and capital costs, reflected in rapidly rising rates, seem to have shifted the political advantage from the utilities to ratepayers. Today, well-organized and well-funded consumer groups often participate in the ratemaking process through rate hearings and legislative lobbying efforts. Groups like Fair Share, Acorn, and the Public Interest Research Group have chapters in many of the fifty states and regularly challenge all or part of a utility's request for rate relief.[3]

Such organized consumer pressure is likely to increase further with the growth in the Ralph Nader-inspired citizen utility boards (CUBs). Conceptually, CUBs are independent consumer groups authorized by state legislatures to speak out at rate cases and on legislative proposals. Their financing is generated by a solicitation distributed with monthly utility bills. Today, the only active CUB is in Wisconsin, but there is pressure to establish them in twenty five other states.[4]

Also under consumer group pressure, many states have designated an office or department within the bureaucracy to represent consumer interests during rate hearings. The attorney-general's office in Massachusetts, for example, regularly intervenes on behalf of consumers. The North Carolina and West Virginia PUCs have divisions to represent consumers, while Maryland, Ohio, Connecticut, and Missouri have their own offices of consumers' counsel. Besides direct political pressure from organizations, consumer dissatisfaction is also manifested by surges of mail and telephone calls to regulators and legislators and by street demonstrations; such activities often follow front-page coverage of PUC announcements to increase rates.

The existence of political pressures does not, of course, guarantee that PUCs will yield to consumers. Indeed, the PUCs' regulatory mandate specifies only legal criteria for deciding rate cases: So long as utilities provide reliable service at the lowest possible cost, rates should be set so that the utilities are allowed to earn a fair and reasonable return and can maintain their financial integrity. In reality, though, political pressures may intrude. Several characteristics of PUCs' political environments make them potentially vulnerable to such pressures.

3. Fair Share and Public Interest Research Group are publicly funded citizen-action organizations. Acorn (Association of Community Organizations for Reform Now) is a nonpartisan, grassroots community organization.

4. Michael de Courcy Hinds, "Citizen Utility Boards Hunt Industry White Elephants," *New York Times* (June 6, 1982).

The four important characteristics are the method of selecting commissioners, the length of commissioners' terms, the source of PUC funding, and the degree of a state's petroleum dependence.[5]

Elected versus Appointed Commissioners

In nine states, commissioners are elected by the general public; in thirty four states, commissioners are appointed, typically by the governor with approval by one or both houses of the legislature or an executive council.

For a number of reasons, political pressures from ratepayers (read "voters") are likely to be greater when commissioners are directly elected. Commissioner-candidates know that campaign promises to hold rates down are likely to woo ratepayer votes, and once in office commissioners have to worry about reelection. Because elections are held every three to six years and power plants take eight to twelve years to build, the benefits of allowing utilities higher returns so that they can undertake capital investment programs typically are not felt before commissioners' terms expire. This short-term political horizon is reinforced by the tendency of consumers to focus more on the immediate costs to them than on the future rewards when evaluating commissioners' performances. Thus, in states where commissioners are directly elected, candidates tend to promise no or low rate hikes. The more rates rise, the more appeal such promises have to consumers.

The success of Billy Lovett, who ascended to a seat on the Georgia PUC on the strength of his populist promises to deny the Georgia Power Company a single additional dollar of rate relief, attests to the appeal of such pledges. This kind of politicking is especially acute when PUC commissioners use the post as a springboard to higher office. The best-known example of this is in Louisiana, where "The Kingfish" Huey Long launched his political rise to the governorship from a seat on the PUC. The list of PUC commissioners who have gone on to higher office does not end there. Senator Paula Hawkins, a former Florida commissioner, based her campaign on her experience as a commissioner and her record of holding rates down.

The problems of using a PUC position as a stepping stone are obvious: Would-be governors don't alienate voters by raising rates, and by the time the results of rate suppression are felt, those who held

5. This discussion is based on my article, "Public Utility Commission Regulation: Perform-ance, Determinants, and Energy Policy Impacts," *Energy Journakl* (March/April 1982): 119.

rates down are long gone from the PUC (e.g., to the Senate) and thus do not have to deal with the consequences.

Appointing rather than electing PUC commissioners helps insulate them from political pressures; but the appointment process does not eliminate all such pressure, because the governors and legislators who do the appointing are often held accountable at the ballot box. Indeed, in the 1970s and early 1980s, utility issues were prominent in a number of gubernatorial elections. Former New Hampshire governor Meldrim Thomson saw his political fortunes crash in a 1978 reelection bid because he supported the use of construction work in progress (CWIP) in rate setting, a controversial PUC policy often advocated by utility interests as necessary to help offset the devastating financial effects of rate suppression. Thomson's successor, Hugh Gallen, proceeded to appoint as chairman of the New Hampshire PUC Michael Love, a well-known consumer advocate and former member of the legislative Utility Consumers Council. That and other similar appointments shifted the entire regulatory climate of the state toward consumer interests.

A similar shift in the regulatory climate occurred at the Texas PUC, which formerly was ranked among the least rate-suppressive by Wall Street. The catalyst for the change in that state was the expiration of numerous contracts between its utilities and natural gas companies. These long-term contracts had been signed years before the energy crisis and stipulated the sale of natural gas to the utilities for as little as 22 cents per thousand cubic feet (mcf). When the contracts expired, gas prices jumped seventeenfold to more than three dollars per mcf. Neither the PUC nor the utility had the power to hold down such increases. The result was a dramatic rise in ratepayers' bills through the fuel-adjustment clause mechanism. In 1982 Mark White successfully challenged Bill Clements for the governorship largely on the strength of promises to hold down utility rates. White has subsequently appointed a number of consumer advocates to the PUC, and the Texas regulatory climate is becoming increasingly rate-suppressive.

Length of Term

The length of commissioners' terms in office also determines the susceptibility of a PUC to political pressure. Today, terms range from three to ten years, with six years the usual stay. Thirty-four states have six-year terms, while twelve states have four-year terms.

The longer the term of office, the less exposed a commissioner is to political pressure, because he or she does not have to go to the electorate or to the governor as often for job renewal. A long term also means that the benefits of unpopular but prudent rate increase decisions made early in a term have time to surface, so a commissioner serving a longer term is more likely to make decisions that pay off over the long run. Recall from the previous chapter that the costs of rate suppression do not hit until several years later. Only after a similar period of time do the benefits of proper regulation begin to accrue. Also, the longer the term, the more time the electorate has to forget an unpopular rate increase.

Source of Funding

A third source of political pressure on PUCs relates to their source of funding. In nineteen states, utilities are assessed fees to finance all regulatory commission activities. In the remaining states, taxpayer funds from the general revenues finance some or all of the commission's activities. From the standpoint of political pressure, assessment funding is preferable to general revenue funding because, in the latter case, state legislators have more influence over the PUC's budget—and, collectively, the PUC. For example, if a state legislator is under pressure from consumer advocates in his or her district to force the PUC to minimize rate hikes, that legislator is far more likely to sway PUC commissioners if the PUC's salaries, staffing levels, and equipment appropriations can be directly influenced next year by that legislator. Even with assessment funding, political pressure remains because some PUCs must still go to the legislature for approval on how funds will be spent. More indirectly, if PUC funding comes out of the general revenues, its budget is more likely to be vulnerable to across-the-board cuts that arise in periods of austerity and government cutbacks, such as those witnessed in the last decade of Proposition 13-type movements.

Petroleum Dependence

A final source of political pressure is dependency on petroleum for electricity generation. The problem here stems not from the use of oil or gas itself but from the tremendous cost increases in these two fuels over the past decade. These rapid rises, which are typically passed immediately to consumers through fuel adjustment clauses, have spurred better organization among consumers, provoked angry letters and calls, and helped make utility regulation an issue in gubernatorial elections, as the foregoing discussion has suggested.

INSTITUTIONAL PRESSURES

While the capture model sheds light on the political underpinnings of rate suppression, a second theory of regulation known as the government-failure model provides insight into the institutional pressures bearing down on PUCs.[6] The basic premise of this model is optimistic in the sense that it assumes that regulators *intend* to serve the public interest; despite these good intentions, however, regulators sometimes fail to reach their objective because of bureaucratic or institutional obstacles.

Massachusetts Institute of Technology economist Paul L. Joskow has provided perhaps the best application of this government failure model to the electric utility industry.[7] According to Joskow, the institutional stage for rate suppression was set in the halcyon decades prior to the 1970s. As Joskow recounts it, rate hearings were few and far between because during that period consumers watched their bills steadily drop, even as utilities raised dividends. Indeed, in this half century utilities often did not file for a new rate for five years or longer, and when they did, it was not uncommon for them to ask for a rate *decrease*. As a result of this low volume of rate cases, PUC commissioners enjoyed a relatively quiet life, and their commissions tended to be sleepy little backwaters in the government bureaucracy where few toiled and few taxpayer dollars were spent.

As discussed in Chapter 1, that peace was broken in the late 1960s and the 1970s by a series of four exogenous shocks to the costs of generating electricity. These four shocks—roller-coaster inflation that began under the Johnson administration, environmental regulations

6. For more on this model, see Peter Navarro, *The Policy Game* (New York: John Wiley & Sons, 1984).

7. Paul L. Joskow, "Inflation and Environmental Concern: Structural Change in the Process of Public Utility Price Regulation," *Journal of Law and Economics* (October 1974): 291.

that raised the cost of power plants by as much as 25 percent, the OPEC oil price hikes, and increased regulatory costs in the wake of Three Mile Island—dramatically raised the costs of energy and capital to electric utilities and created enormous pressures for rapid rate increases.

As Joskow recounts it, the PUCs were caught ill-prepared for these inflationary shocks and the increased demand for their services. Instead of seeing a utility file a rate case once every five years, many PUCs began to see them filed as often as every year. Indeed, over the last decade, the number of rate cases PUCs have been called on to decide each year has increased greatly.

For example, in 1970 the number of rate cases filed nationwide totaled only 80, but in the year of the Arab oil embargo that number jumped to 212. Since that time, the number of cases has been consistently double or more than the 80-case 1970 benchmark, with cases in 1980 hitting a record 254.[8] From 1979 to 1981 alone, decisions on rate cases jumped by 56 percent. Today, three major institutional factors make the PUCs potentially susceptible to government failure in the form of rate suppression.

Budgets and Staffs

As a rule, PUC budgets and staffs are too small to process rate cases in a timely way. Yesteryear's occasional applications for a rate decrease required only small staffs, meager budgets, and little more than a hand calculator to process the cases. Unfortunately, when the number of rate cases began growing exponentially, many PUCs could not keep up with their new workloads. Lack of foresight was part of the problem, but, as our earlier discussion has indicated, taxpayer resistance to expanding *any* government bureaucracy, much less the one responsible for their soaring electricity bills, has also played a part.

Thus, although the regulatory bodies of some states like New York and California have managed to grow with the times, most PUCs remain woefully understaffed and underbudgeted. Also, few commissions have been able to invest in new computer technology, which could greatly offset their limitations in staff. The bottom line is that rate cases tend to pile up in regulators' in-boxes, exacerbating one of

---

8. Scott A. Fenn, *America's Electric Utilities* (Washington, D.C.: Investor Responsibility Research Center, 1983), p. 40.

the primary causes of rate suppression, regulatory lag. Such a lag has meant that even when a rate hike is granted in full, a utility still may not earn its market costs of generating electricity, because by the time the increase goes into effect, inflation has already eaten away some of the value of the rate hike.

Salary Structure

In most PUCs, commissioners and their staffs are grossly underpaid. Because their salaries are generally below those for similar positions in federal regulatory agencies and far below those in regulated companies, many PUCs are unable to attract and *keep* the professionals required to run the commission properly. It is typical for PUCs to be able to attract young, bright but inexperienced people who, after several years of apprenticeship, double their salaries by moving on to jobs in federal agencies or utility companies. This headhunting problem applies also to commissioners.

Commissioner's Qualifications

Poorly qualified commissioners are a third potential contributor to government failure. Today PUCs face complex issues that cross a broad range of subjects: law, economics, engineering, and accounting Ideally, commissions should bring together people with backgrounds in these different areas of expertise. Unfortunately, only nine states have legislative statutes requiring that some or all of their PUC commissioners be professionally qualified. The Rhode Island statute sets a good example: "Commissioners will be selected with regard to their qualifications in law and government, economics and finance, engineering and accounting." But the professional qualification oversight by the majority of states leaves the door open to candidates unsuited for the job, particularly where commissioners are elected. In such states, the lay commissioner tends to be more the rule than the exception. It is precisely such an oversight that created the opportunity for the aforementioned Commissioner Lovett—a former race car driver—to set electricity rates in Georgia.

Merely using the ratemaking formula itself requires an understanding of very complex accounting procedures that are unique to the industry. Concepts such as "construction work in progress," "allowance for funds used during construction," and the "normalization" versus "flow-through" of tax benefits are but the tip of an iceberg that only a highly trained professional can fathom. Similarly, to rule on whether or not to approve construction of a new power plant requires some knowledge of the economist's forecasting tools and mastery of economic concepts such as elasticities and interfuel substitutes, while the seemingly simple calculation of fuel expenses requires an understanding of such basic engineering concepts as heat rates and thermal efficiencies. Even the most highly qualified and trained candidates must spend several years on the commission to learn the intricacies and idiosyncracies of the ratemaking process.

The Ratemaking Formula

A final institutional problem is the ratemaking formula itself. This formula is the artifact of an earlier era of steadily falling unit costs of producing electricity. To become suited to the task at hand (coping with inflation), it requires major modifications.[9] These changes include mechanisms like the "future test year" (which anticipates inflation), "attrition allowances" (which offset the erosion of earnings by regulatory lag), and "levelizing rates" to moderate the impact of rate increases.

Besides the political problems, there are other kinds of obstacles preventing the adoption of such mechanisms. A more complicated formula would require computers and more sophisticated personnel to operate them, but the budgets and qualifications of commissioners constrain many PUCs and reinforce the status quo. For example, utilities in Massachusetts have for years been pushing the PUC to install a "future test year" to cope with inflation. The primary reason why this innovation has been rejected in previous years is that the chairman of the commission thought that he simply did not have the staff and equipment to monitor such a reform. He claimed that "the calculations would be too complex."[10]

9. For discussion, see Peter Navarro, Bruce C. Peterson, and Thomas R. Stauffer, "A Critical Comparison of Utility-type Ratemaking Methodologies in Oil Pipeline Regulation," *Bell Journal of Economics* (Autumn 1981): 392.

10. Personal communication from Jon Bonsall, former chairman of the DPU.

IDEOLOGICAL PRESSURES

The ideological dimensions of rate suppression are by far the most controversial. (As defined here, a person's ideology or political philosophy consists of a fairly consistent set of values and beliefs about how the world is and should be.) A third model of regulation, the ideological model, helps explain this controversy.[11]

The ideological model of regulation shares the basic premise of the government failure model, namely, that regulators seek to serve the public interest. But it differs from that model in that it gives regulators more credit for having the ability to overcome institutional barriers. The important contribution the model makes is that it allows for different interpretations of "the public good." According to the model, two regulators can pursue two totally different policies, each of which is believed to be in the public interest. For example, a conservative regulator might favor the abolition of oil or gas price controls because they are inefficient ("we need more petroleum, and price controls discourage new exploration and drilling"), while a liberal regulator might support controls on equity grounds ("poor consumers must be protected from rapacious, rich petroleum companies").

In the ideological view, rate suppression is not a Machiavellian plot by consumers (as proponents of the capture theory insist) or an institutional failure but rather a means by which regulators pursue their own concept of the public interest. The traditional conservative/liberal split over property rights versus redistribution and the more recent ideological conflict that emerged in the late 1960s between advocates of economic growth and expounders of a "small is beautiful" philosophy help shed light on this public interest view of rate suppression.

The role of regulation in income redistribution is well known. As previously indicated, natural gas price controls benefit gas consumers at the expense of gas producers, airline regulation once benefited the major airlines at the expense of air travelers, and so on. In the case of utility regulation, the redistributional struggle is between ratepayers and shareholders. As we have seen, rate suppression effects a very subtle form of redistribution: It *blocks* the trans-

---

11. The origin of this model can be traced to the work of Harvard economist Joseph P. Kalt. Kalt actually combined the capture and ideology models in a capture-ideology formula. See also Navarro, *The Policy Game.*

fer of billions of dollars from consumers to utility shareholders by denying utilities their market costs of generating electricity.[12]

Conservatives tend to oppose such redistribution on the grounds that it represents an unfair confiscation of utility shareholders' property. This confiscation takes place in the form of a devaluation of utility stock as a consequence of rate suppression.

Liberals, on the other hand, tend to support redistributive rate suppression on the grounds that utility shareholders are, on average, wealthier than the average ratepayer. Under this assumption, it is therefore more fair to let utility shareholders bear a disproportionate share of the rising costs of energy and capital. In this view, rate suppression serves a function similar to that of a progressive income tax, that is, to promote a more even and therefore "more equitable" distribution of income.

Through the ideological lens, rate suppression can also be viewed as a debate over a world of economic growth versus one of low or zero growth. Pro-growthers see a steady expansion of the economy as the key to raising the real incomes of all Americans. They claim that capital expansion in the electric utility industry is absolutely necessary for the industry to supply the electricity needed to support the nation's economic growth. Such capital expansion tends to take the form of large, central-station power plants that are predominantly coal- or nuclear-fired. While those who advocate the "hard path" of electricity expansion recognize the potential air pollution and safety hazards associated with these types of plants, they believe that the risks must be borne as an unfortunate but necessary trade-off for low electricity costs.

In contrast, the low-growthers or no-growthers envision a "soft path" of electricity provision, one in which large, unsightly, unclean, and unsafe central-station fossil and nuclear plants must give way to decentralized wind generators, solar cells, geothermal resources, biomass, and the like. Some factions within this "small is beautiful" contingent see such a soft path as not only safer but also more economic. They believe that in an era of rising capital costs, it is

---

12. A more explicit form of PUC redistribution is the use of lifeline rates, whereby utility shareholders and electricity consumers as a group subsidize the rates of a subgroup of consumers, the poor and the elderly.

cheaper to invest in smaller, less capital-intensive projects.[13] The Environmental Defense Fund, for example, intervened in a number of rate cases to argue for a construction program that relies on such alternative energy systems as solar, geothermal, and end-use conservation in place of large coal and nuclear plants.[14] These PUC challenges were unique in that the EDF used actual ratemaking models to illustrate the economic superiority of its proposed alternative.[15] Still other factions of the soft-path movement say that while decentralization and soft-path technologies might cost more, that higher cost is a price worth paying for a safer, cleaner, more attractive plant. Thus, in the "small is beautiful" view of the world, rate suppression is useful for preventing electric utilities from investing in large central-station power plants. In other words, rate suppression achieves the ideological goal by forcing the utilities into a strategy of capital minimization.

THE POLITICS OF RATE SUPPRESSION: A STATISTICAL TEST

To test the relative importance of these political, institutional, and ideological factors in leading state PUCs to adopt rate-suppressive policies, I conducted a study for the Department of Energy.[16] Table 8-1 ranks the state PUCs on the basis of their propensity to suppress rates.[17] These rankings were statistically related to eight of the measures of the political, institutional, and ideological forces discussed above. The results of that statistical test lend strong support to the idea

13. For more on the soft path, see Amory B. Lovins, *Soft Energy Paths* (Cambridge, Mass.: Ballinger, 1977), also published by Friends of the Earth; and Roger W. Sant, "Least Cost Energy Strategy: Minimizing Consumer Costs Through Competition," Mellon Institute Energy Productivity Center, Virg., 1979 (55), special report.

14. See, for example, Testimony of W.R.Z. Willey, staff economist, Environmental Defense Fund, Inc., before the California Public Utilities Commission, "Alternative Energy Systems for Pacific Gas & Electric Co.," 1978.

15. The results were, however, contested because of the assumptions about capital and fuel costs that were fed into the model; controversy continues about the economic advantage of the soft over the hard path. For a discussion, see Howard W. Pifer III, William H. Hierongmus, Joel M. Ristuccia, and Michael M. Schnitzer, "An Independent Evaluation of EDF's Electric Utility Financial Simulation Model" (Cambridge: Putnam, Hayes & Bartlett, Joint Hearing of OII-26 and OII-42 before the California Public Utilities Commission, undated).

16. The results are reported in Navarro, "Public Utility Commission Regulation."

17. These rankings are based on the assessments of five investment or research firms: Goldman Sachs, Salomon Brothers, Valueline, Merrill Lynch, and Duff and Phelps.

Table 8–1.   State PUCs Ranked by Their Propensity to Suppress Rates.

Least Rate Suppressive	Moderate Rate Suppression	Most Rate Suppressive
Arizona	Arkansas	Alabama
Florida	Colorado	California
Hawaii	Delaware	Connecticut
Indiana	District of Columbia	Georgia
New Mexico	Idaho	Iowa
North Carolina	Illinois	Louisiana
Texas	Kansas	Maine
Utah	Kentucky	Massachusetts
Wisconsin	Maryland	Mississippi
	Michigan	Missouri
	Minnesota	Montana
	Nevada	North Dakota
	New Hampshire	Rhode Island
	New Jersey	South Dakota
	New York	West Virginia
	Ohio	
	Oklahoma	
	Oregon	
	Pennsylvania	
	South Carolina	
	Vermont	
	Virginia	
	Washington	
	Wyoming	

Source: This is a composite ranking developed from the rankings of Goldman Sachs, Merrill Lynch, Salomon Brothers, Valueline, and Duff and Phelps. Alaska, Tennessee, and Nebraska are typically not ranked.

that all three of these forces cause rate suppression.

For example, PUCs with directly elected commissioners were found to be the most likely to be rate suppressive. Specifically, for an "otherwise average PUC" (based on the sample mean), a shift from an appointed to an elected commission increased political pressures and thereby raised the probability of rate suppression by 48 points.

Similarly, an institutional measure, salary level, was the third most important determinant of rate suppression. Reducing salaries 15 percent below the mean raised the probability of an unfavorable rank by 25 points, while movement to a more ideologically liberal commission raised the probability of rate suppression by 19 points.

More generally, the length of commissioner terms, the method of funding PUCs, the percentage of oil in a state's generation mix, the PUC budget size, and the presence or absence of requirements that PUC commissioners be legally qualified for the job all had significant effects on the probability of rate suppression, and these effects were all in the direction expected. Accordingly, the test illustrates that PUC regulatory failure is rooted in all three theoretical explanations— political, institutional, and ideological. The importance of these findings is that they suggest a number of constructive policy reforms to eliminate rate suppression, which the next and final chapter illustrates.

9 A POLICY BLUEPRINT FOR A BRIGHT FUTURE

The rate-suppression/capital-minimization syndrome threatens to disrupt our economy. The dimming of America in the literal sense seems unlikely, but in an economic and figurative sense it looms in the form of higher consumer rates for less reliable service, continued overdependence on foreign energy, decreased national security, and reduction in economic growth, real income, and employment.

A far brighter alternative electricity future can be ensured, however, if a number of constructive policy reforms are taken at the state level to eliminate or moderate the political and institutional forces driving the PUCs to suppress rates; the ideological dimensions of rate suppression must likewise be addressed. At the same time, the federal government has an important role to play in ensuring that the states do indeed undertake the PUC reforms that are in the best interest of national policy goals; it also has a responsibility to eliminate or reduce the often needless inflationary pressure it has imposed on the utility industry, its customers, and its regulators through its fiscal irresponsibility and regulatory hurdles. The remainder of this chapter is dedicated to explaining the state and federal policy options.

STATE PUC REFORMS

To alleviate political pressure, states should consider appointing,

111

rather than electing, their PUC commissioners. Even in states where commissioners are currently appointed, legislatures should consider a reform of the appointment procedure to further reduce political pressure on the governors who typically are charged with selecting commissioners. In this regard, Florida provides a model approach for minimizing such political pressure. Specifically, the Florida statute specifies that a panel drawn from both houses of the legislature conduct a search for qualified candidates for commissioner; the governor then is allowed to choose from a list of qualified people.[1]

If this appointment procedure were combined with longer terms— equal at least to the eight to fourteen years it takes to build a power plant today—commissioners might enjoy sufficient insulation from day-to-day politics to make unpopular but prudent choices when necessary. As final buffers against political pressure, the PUCs should be financed primarily through assessments on utilities rather than through general tax revenues, and state legislatures should provide their commissions with more autonomy in determining the size of their budget and how that money is spent.

To reduce the prospect of institutional failure, state legislatures should raise the salaries for both commissioners and their staffs to levels that are competitive with those for similar positions in government and industry. At the same time, states should require that commissioners demonstrate competence in law, engineering, accounting, or economics. Such reforms will assure that highly qualified people are attracted to and placed in PUC positions and, more important, by eliminating the "headhunting problem" through higher salaries, will ensure that these people remain in the job. PUC budgets should also be generous enough to allow the hiring of sufficient staff and the purchase of new computer technology so that rate cases can be processed rapidly enough to avoid the hazards of regulatory lag.

IDEOLOGY AND THE SMART PATH

Dealing with the ideological dimensions of rate suppression is less straightforward. A major problem is that people often react emotionally when their political philosophies are challenged. In the case of

1. Florida Statutes ch. 350.031 ("Florida Public Service Commission Nominating Council").

redistributive rate suppression, the problem lies not so much with the *goal* of a more equitable distribution of income but rather with the *means* to achieve it. Put simply, PUC regulation is simply too blunt a tool to transfer wealth from the richer to the poorer, because people of all income levels are ratepayers. More important, over the longer term, rate suppression actually makes everyone worse off. Thus, using PUC regulation as a redistributive tool, no matter how well intended, inevitably backfires. The enlightened liberal will recognize this and seek more direct and targeted means of cushioning the poor and the elderly from the crunch of rapidly rising electricity bills. Such measures might include electricity stamps, cash subsidies, and changes in the income tax structure. Seeking such measures will have the added benefit of bringing the redistribution debate out into the open rather than masking it behind the issue of "fair" electricity regulation.

If we are to avoid the consequences of ideological rate suppression, we must also challenge those who advocate keeping rates artificially low as a means for ensuring low or zero growth. A "small is beautiful" world is not cost-free. If zero or low growth is to be the goal, we must be willing to accept the attendant high costs—reduced economic prosperity, lower real income, fewer jobs—that a strategy of capital minimization entails. And we should also realize that those who will bear a large share of these costs are average Americans searching for a better standard of living and poorer Americans already hard-pressed to find a job and pay their utility bills.

Moreover, a point that has been totally lost in the economic analyses of the soft-path energy options is that rate suppression not only denies utilities the capital to build large fossil-fuel and nuclear plants but it prohibits investment in conservation and in such alternative energy sources as wind, solar, and geothermal power as well. In other words, rate suppression precludes taking the hard path of constructing large central-station power plants and thereby meets a goal of zero growth. But at the same time and contrary to the zero-growth philosophy, it prevents utilities from pursuing soft-path alternatives to their present generating facilities. For the nation, the only *smart path* is one in which utilities have the financial capabilities to pursue a mix of hard- and soft-path options that takes the best from both worlds.[2]

2. See Peter Navarro, "The Soft, Hard, or Smart Path: Charting the Electric Utility Industry's Future," *Public Utilities Fortnightly* (June 18, 1981): 25.

THE FEDERAL ROLE

If the states fail to adopt the above policy reforms, the federal government has both the right and the responsibility to step in with its own solutions. While critics may charge that such an intrusion is a violation of states' rights, the potential problems created by PUC rate suppression go far beyond state borders and spill over into important national energy, security, and economic policy goals. Any federal intervention must, however, be a prudent one that will solve old problems rather than create new ones. Discussion of the four major options open to the federal government—nationalization of regulation, regionalization, a federal standards approach, and deregulation—points out both the problems and promise of each alternative.

Nationalizing regulation means that the federal government would take charge of regulating utilities. This idea is probably more useful as a threat to force state regulatory reform than as a workable solution. The Federal Energy Regulatory Commission (FERC), which regulates the sales of electric power among utility companies, is the most likely agency to assume the regulatory responsibilities the state PUCs now have. But FERC has neither the staff nor the resources to handle such a heavy workload. Besides, Wall Street considers the FERC to be at least as rate-suppressive as a majority of the state PUCs.[3] Under its stewardship, regulatory performance thus might improve in some very rate-suppressive states, but in other states rate suppression might get worse.

Regionalizing electric utility regulation would be a much more useful approach. By setting up commissions on a regional basis but letting states have representation by allowing them to appoint their own commissioners, the government could preserve a degree of state control over state-based utilities while creating a structure that more closely parallels that of a national electricity generation and delivery system. Regional coordination also would provide a system that is better equipped to cope with the kinds of energy shortages that resulted from the oil embargo of 1973–74 and the 109-day coal strike of 1978. Most utilities now provide electricity on an interstate basis, and many are organized into sophisticated regional power pools that help minimize the costs of electricity through the sharing of power. Yet

3. Peter Navarro, "Electric Utility Regulation and National Energy Policy," *Regulation* (January/February 1981): 20.

state PUCs rarely communicate or coordinate their activities with one another. Congress could either mandate that states organize regional regulatory commissions or create them itself.

That this is a potentially constructive reform is suggested by a recent resolution passed by the National Governors' Association calling for federal legislation to enable states to join together to regionally coordinate utility planning and system coordination. The proposal "reflects the fact that state authorities realize that substantial structural reform of electric power regulation may be required to ensure the long-term sufficiency and efficiency of electric supplies."[4]

Still a third approach that could be used in combination with regionalization is to *set federal standards* that the PUCs must adopt. The Reagan administration has already partially done this in its 1982 Economic Recovery Act, which requires state PUCs to adopt the normalization of tax benefits in order to be eligible for federal tax subsidies to state utilities. More broadly, such standards as allowing construction work in progress (CWIP) in the rate base, using a future test year to calculate rates, and limiting regulatory lag (for example, by allowing a maximum of six months for consideration of rate hikes, as Massachusetts has done) would help moderate the effects of rate suppression. The precedent for a federal-guidelines approach already exists in the Public Utility Reform and Policy Act of 1978, which set up five ratemaking and six regulatory standards for state PUCs.[5]

Finally, there is the *deregulation* option, which has recently been the focus of much interest and debate.[6] Interest in this approach has grown out of the broader deregulation debate that began in the 1970s and resulted in an unprecedented dismantling of the federal regulatory house. Airlines, banking, trucking, and oil prices have all been deregulated recently and, by most accounts, with great success. It is therefore not surprising that deregulation has been proposed as a way out of the rate-suppression trap. In weighing the deregulation option, however, it is important to bear in mind several unique features of the utility industry that may limit the effectiveness of this policy approach.

First, unlike the airlines, trucking, and banking industries, the utility industry faces a serious natural-monopoly problem. As dis-

---

4. *The Future of Electric Power in America* (Washington, D.C.: U.S. Department of Energy, Office of Policy, Planning, and Analysis, June 1983), p. ES–25.

5. The Public Utility Regulatory Policies Act of 1978 (PURPA), P.L. 95-617.

6. For an overview, see MIT economists Paul L. Joskow and Richard Schmalensee, *Markets for Power: An Analysis of Electric Utility Deregulation* (Cambridge, Mass.: MIT Press, 1983).

cussed in Chapter 1, this problem arises because of economies of scale and distribution. These economies mean that one large utility with low costs will typically be able to drive out smaller rivals through predatory pricing; and once these rivals are gone, competition and efficiency may turn into monopolistic waste and profiteering. That this natural-monopoly problem is a serious one is attested to by the fact that no serious policy analyst ever recommends complete deregulation. Instead, current proposals are limited to deregulating electrical *generation*; they leave regulation for the *transmission* and *distribution* of electricity.

The beauty of deregulating electrical generation lies in its potential to eliminate the reliability penalty. As envisioned, a free market in bulk power would spur entrepreneurs to step in and provide the plants necessary to keep the lights on in the future.[7] Even this best-case deregulation scenario, however, fails to deal with the fuel penalty created by rate suppression. It fails primarily because it ignores the substantial opportunities utilities now have to convert existing petroleum plants to coal. Indeed, in most proposals, only *new* capacity would be deregulated.

Besides these limitations of deregulation, there is a far more serious problem, namely, the length of time that it would take to implement it. While such an option came rather quickly to other industries, various legal and regulatory problems peculiar to the utility industry imply an incubation time of a decade or more. Chief among these problems are the common-carrier issue (whether deregulated suppliers would have the right of access to regulated utilities' transmission lines) and the inevitable jurisdictional disputes that will arise among federal, state, and regional entities. There is also an even more intractable problem: valuing the existing assets and obtaining security holders' approval in the case of any scenario that involves setting up a deregulated segment of a currently regulated company.

Thus, while deregulation has certain attractions as a long-term experiment, it is clearly not *the* solution to the problems of rate suppression that must be dealt with right away.[8]

7. It is useful to bear in mind that there is a strong counterargument that concludes that no new central-station power plants would be built in a deregulated environment. On this point, see Mitnick & Associates, "Competitive Entry of New Powerplants" (study for the Pennsylvania Governor's Energy Council, March 1983).

8. As utility analyst Scott A. Fenn has remarked, deregulation "appears exceedingly unlikely in view of the prodigious economic, political, legal, and financial obstacles to such a move." *America's Electric Utilities* (Washington, D.C.: Investor Responsibility Research Center, 1983), p. 90.

Moving beyond these regulatory policies, the federal government must get its fiscal and monetary policy house in order. Large budget deficits that push up interest rates and "crowd out" the private sector from the capital markets or spur inflation can only exacerbate the rate-suppression/capital-minimization syndrome. In contrast, keeping budget deficits, interest rates, and inflation low will take away much of the need for frequent rate hikes, while private-sector capital spending will spur growth both within the utility industry and other sectors far more effectively than will government spending.

At the same time, a thorough reform of the licensing and environmental pollution-control procedures for new power plants could greatly decrease the time it takes to construct such plants and thus lower their real costs (by reducing the cost of capital penalty).

Finally, the federal government is the most logical entity to promote a better understanding of the electric utility problem and its ramifications for consumer and national welfare. This it can do through more aggressive public information programs conducted under the auspices of agencies such as the Department of Energy. Increased public understanding will do much to reduce the vulnerability of public opinion to the demagoguery that has all too often enshrouded utility rate and construction issues. It will also help pave the way for constructive policy reforms.

In summary, there are many constructive reforms that policymakers can pursue at both the state and federal levels. Ultimately, any success at implementing these reforms—and ending the dangers of rate suppression—depends not only on an informed policymaking community but also on a supportive public.

To this end, electricity consumers must become aware that ostensibly pro-consumer rate suppression is working against their longer term interests as well as the national interest. The message that rates should be higher now to hold rate hikes down in the future is not, however, an easy one to accept. This bitter pill does become a bit easier to swallow when electricity rate increases are looked at not as money down the drain but as an investment in the nation's infrastructure, national security, and economic prosperity. That message, however, is now totally lost in the debate over rising electricity rates.

AFTERWORD

My hope is that this book will rekindle a major policy debate over the future of the electric utility industry. Such a debate began in earnest in the mid- to late-1970s when the symptoms of rate suppression began to show. That debate was supposed to culminate in a major policy initiative by the Reagan administration in 1983 that would have addressed many of the underlying regulatory as well as financial problems of the industry.

Unfortunately, the administration's Electricity Policy Project was put on the back burner. Part of the reason lay in the "changing of the guard" at the agency directing the project (the Department of Energy), but recent events in the oil markets, the world economy, and electricity demand growth have worked to foster four beliefs now widely shared in Washington that also helped kill the initiative.[1] These beliefs are (1) that the era of rate suppression—and all its attendant problems—is over; (2) that future petroleum prices will be much lower than many experts expect; (3) that growth in electricity demand will, likewise, be

1. The Electricity Policy Project had the strong support of DOE Secretary James Edwards. When Edwards was replaced by current Secretary Donald Hodel, there was first a long delay in the release of the project's results and then a radical watering down of its message: Rather than becoming a policy document to be used to propose legislation, the project became simply a descriptive report of the scope of the problem. See *The Future of Electric Power in America* (Washington, D.C.: U.S. Department of Energy, Office of Policy, Planning, and Analysis, June 1983).

119

below expectations; and (4) that lower price trajectories for oil and gas mean that displacing those fuels is no longer economically advantageous.

On the surface, the first belief appears to have some merit. Oil prices have dropped from their previous highs, and the rate of growth in the real price of electricity appears to have, at least temporarily, slowed considerably. At the same time, a worldwide recession coupled with the Reagan economic program has put the brakes on inflation. Thus, according to this view, two of the major sources of upward pressure on electricity rates—higher energy and capital costs—have moderated; therefore, the argument runs, rate suppression is no longer a problem.

If these changes are permanent, then regulatory rate suppression may indeed be over. Unfortunately, this does *not* mean that the *effects* of rate suppression will necessarily disappear. The behavior of utility industry executives indicates that they do not anticipate a permanent reduction of inflationary forces. Any expectation of a renewed bout of inflation is likely to cause an experienced utility executive to continue with a capital-averse strategy, and for a very good reason. While the forces bearing on the regulatory mechanism may have temporarily moderated, no comprehensive reform of that process has been undertaken to insulate utilities from future increases in inflation. Thus, the rational utility executive realizes that rate suppression will rear its head every time inflationary pressures return and therefore sticks with a capital minimization strategy, even in the face of a temporary abatement of energy and capital cost inflation. This strategy is evident in the fact that utility executives still are refusing (or are financially unable) to undertake economic coal conversions, to pursue conservation to its full economic promise, or to build sufficient new plants to meet anticipated load growth.

The point is that the mere possibility of a renewal of inflation is sufficient to ensure the consequences of rate suppression, even if we do not observe depressed utility returns. To avoid these consequences we must reform the regulatory mechanism in ways that remove the sources of rate suppression.[2]

What about the second belief, that petroleum prices will be much lower than many experts expect? A sustained deflation of oil prices would indeed turn much of the fuel penalty into a fuel bonus.

---

2. The Department of Energy takes an even less sanguine view of recent events. Its Electricity Policy Project study concludes that despite a lessening of inflation, "the utility industry still faces substantial financial disincentives for new investment." *Future of Electric Power*, p. ES-20.

No one can refute this argument once and for all without gazing into a crystal ball. But the possibility of tumult like that in the Middle East over the last decade, coupled with the world's apparent voracious appetite for oil, leads most analysts to expect, at best, zero escalation in real petroleum prices and, at worst, a return to the galloping increases of the 1970s. The hope, then, of dramatic deflation occupies a small corner of the probability distribution, and counting on such a future entails high risk.

The third belief centers around lower load growth. Reduced growth in demand for electricity could happen through several channels. The most promising channel is conservation beyond current expectations. The most menacing channel is a continuation of world recession. Either or both events would reduce the need for new power plant construction to keep the lights on. But note that this would be primarily for *reliability* reasons.

The important point here (other than the fact that few forecasters expect a zero or negative load growth) is that some utility investment would *still* be economic in a low load-growth world. It would still be economic to convert or replace existing petroleum plants with alternative fuels such as coal. Only lower load growth *plus* a deflation in petroleum prices would eliminate the need for utility investment in anything but replacement plants. Because most arguments for lower load growth hinge on *higher* oil prices (to stimulate conservation), this dual good fortune is unlikely enough that some capital investment should always be economic.[3]

Finally, there is the belief that lower price trajectories projected for oil and gas mean that new nonpetroleum power plant construction or coal conversion to displace these fuels is no longer economic. Nothing could be further from the truth. As the DOE Electricity Policy Project concluded:

> There still remains a substantial economic benefit from displacing oil or natural gas as a baseload generation fuel with either new coal-fired or nuclear facilities. . . . Over 200 delays or cancellations of new coal-fired or nuclear facilities were announced in 1980 and 1981. As many as half of these plants could reduce the cost of electricity by displacing high-cost fuels, and their delay or cancellation will thereby cause electric prices to be higher than necessary. In fact, it is estimated that these delays and cancellations in that two-year period alone will cause consumers to pay

3. There is a counterargument that says that higher oil prices will actually lead to high load growth. In such a case, the gains from conservation will be more than offset by increases in demand from fuel-switching from petroleum to electricity.

$20 billion more for electricity (in net present value, 1982 dollars) over the remainder of this century. Annual electric bills could be as much as $18 billion higher by 2000 if utilities pursue supply strategies intended only to minimize their capital expenditures. Thus, failure to pursue economic investments in new supply will have a substantial adverse impact on electric prices while, at the same time, increasing oil import levels and serving as a damper on economic growth.[4]

Here in the mid-1980s there remains a crying need for a large-scale policy reform of electric utility regulation. The time to act is now, before the dimming of America changes from a remote possibility to a dark reality.

4. *Future of Electric Power*, op. cit., p. ES-12.

INDEX

123

ABOUT THE AUTHOR

Peter Navarro is a researcher at the John F. Kennedy School of Government's Energy and Environmental Policy Center and a teaching fellow at Harvard University. He received a Masters Degree in Public Administration from the Kennedy School in 1979, a Masters Degree in Economics from Harvard University in 1982, and is completing his doctoral dissertation, also at Harvard.

He has served as a staff member of Governor Edward J. King's Task Force on Reform of the Fuel Adjustment Clause, and as an adviser to the Massachusetts Energy Office. He has also testified before Congress and appeared as a speaker and lecturer before a variety of groups. His articles on economics and public policy have appeared in a broad spectrum of publications ranging from the *Wall Street Journal* and the *New York Times* to the *Public Interest*, *Regulation*, the *Energy Law Review*, and the *Harvard Business Review*.